Parent–Teacher Partnership

Practical Approaches to Meet
Special Educational Needs

Mike Blamires, Chris Robertson
and Joanna Blamires

David Fulton Publishers

London

David Fulton Publishers Ltd
Ormond House, 26–27 Boswell Street, London WC1N 3JD

First published in Great Britain by David Fulton Publishers 1997

British Library Cataloguing in Publication Data
A catalogue record for this book is available from the British Library

ISBN 1–85346–470–8

Typeset by Kate Williams, London
Printed in Great Britain by Bell and Bain Ltd, Glasgow

Contents

The Authors

Mike Blamires is the programme director of the Postgraduate Diploma/MA at the special needs research and development centre within the department of education at Canterbury Christ Church College.

Chris Robertson is senior lecturer in special educational needs at the special needs research and development centre within the department of education at Canterbury Christ Church College. His main teaching and research interests are in the area of profound and multiple learning difficulties and physical and neurological impairment. He has had significant teaching experience with children and young people with profound and multiple learning difficulties and physical disabilities. Chris has held senior management posts in special education including being deputy and acting headteacher.

Joanna Blamires is a parent of three children, one of whom has special educational needs. She has been a teacher of children with special needs and now works voluntarily for a parental support group.

We would like to thank all the teachers, parents, professionals and children who have helped us to gain a better understanding of this important and evolving subject.

Introduction

Schools and local educational authorities want flexibility in order to manage their finite resources efficiently and reallocate existing resources to new priorities. Parents want the reassurance that their child's needs are recognised and that the resources needed are being deployed.

The Code of Practice improves on previous legislation by emphasising the importance of parent partnership in meeting a child's special educational needs. In fact the document refers to parents on nearly every page. For partnership to become a reality, an understanding of the constraints that underpin this partnership is vital. In order to outline the limits of parent–teacher partnership, this book has to be negative. By not shying away from the difficulties, we hope to facilitate positive ways forward.

Use this book to prompt discussion about current practice. Photocopy sections that you feel may be useful to promote discussion within your school and among parents with similar concerns about the provision for their children. The review section should help teachers and parents to establish current practice and then to establish priorities for further development. Schools can only develop from where they are now but that does not mean that practice cannot be improved dramatically. Despite conflicts which will always occur due to limited resources, teachers, parents and other professionals will ultimately agree that they are all working for the best interests of the child. This book's intention is to show that more than one viewpoint is important and that the easy answers and assumptions do not always lead to long-term solutions.

How to use this book

Chapter 1

What is Parent–Teacher Partnership?

The relationships between parents of children with special educational needs and the school which their child is attending has a crucial bearing on the child's educational progress and the effectiveness of any school based action.

School based arrangements should ensure that assessment reflects a sound and comprehensive knowledge of a child and his or her responses to a variety of carefully planned and recorded actions which take account of the wishes, feelings and knowledge of parents at all stages.

Children's progress will be diminished if their parents are not seen as partners in the educational process with unique knowledge and information to impart.

Professional help can seldom be wholly effective unless it builds upon parents' capacity to be involved and unless professionals take account of what they say and treat their views and anxieties as intrinsically important.

(DFEE 1994a, 2:28)

Parent–teacher partnership to meet special educational needs is an elaboration and extension of existing whole-school practice in this area.

Partnership implies:
1) Mutual Respect
2) Complementary Expertise
3) A willingness to learn from each other

(Armstrong 1996, p.18)

1

Beyond exhortation and rhetoric

Parent–teacher partnership has risen in importance over the last two decades and much has been written about it. We are slowly moving away from writing about the subject as if it 'would be a good thing' and then adding a mix of rhetoric and exhortation in the hope it would 'get things moving'. As the Code of Practice notes, 'Most schools already have effective working relationships with parents, including the parents of children with special needs' (DFEE 1994a, 2:28). However, it would be unrealistic and a little too idealistic to believe that parent–teacher partnership is just about to blossom. The partnership is developmental and begins time after time when a new child joins the school or a cause for concern is raised in relation to a child. The building of a partnership depends upon a mutual commitment to common priorities. Because resources are finite, special educational needs have to be met through the efficient use of resources.

If there is no common commitment to or even acknowledgement of these priorities by parents, schools or LEAs, then parent–teacher partnership will be built upon shaky foundations. Recent legislation means that there is more likely to be a conflict of interests between all these parties and this has been implicitly recognised by the DFEE through its GEST funding of LEA-based parent partnership schemes in order to cope with sources of potential conflict.

> The knowledge, views and experience of parents are vital. Effective assessment and provision will be secured when there is the greatest possible degree of partnership between parents, and their children, and the schools, LEAs and other agencies.
>
> (DFEE 1994a, 1:2)

If progress is to be made towards parent–teacher partnership then all involved need to be 'frank and open' to make clear the boundaries and expectations that underpin it.

This book is a realistic but positive attempt to move all partners beyond rhetoric and exhortation towards a practical understanding of needs and roles. It does not offer a recipe or even a set of recipes that ensure success. More appropriately, it aims to provide a road map towards successful partnership with signposts to some key destinations and warnings about possible blind alleys.

Where has parent–teacher partnership come from?

In order to understand where conflicts of interests may arise within parent–teacher partnership it is important to understand how the concept has developed and why differing priorities make parent–teacher partnership mean different things to different people.

The legacy of Plowden

The Plowden report (CACE 1967) on primary education in the 1960s recognised the important effect of positive parental attitudes

2

upon educational performance and sought to encourage parental co-operation through a series of recommendations which included:

(I) All schools should have a programme for contact with children's homes to include:

a) a regular system for the head and class teacher to meet parents before the child enters

b) arrangements for more formal private talks preferably twice a year

c) open days to be held at times chosen to enable parents to attend

d) parents to be given booklets prepared by the schools to inform them in their choice of children's school and as to how they are being educated

e) written reports on children to be made at least once a year; the child's work should be seen by parents

f) special efforts to make contact with parents who do not visit schools.

(CACE 1967)

The basic groundwork for partnership was thus set and thirty years later schools are still grappling with item f). The concept of partnership was in the context of schools being a resource for the community. A school could have a role to play in improving the lot of a community and it was the professional's job to improve identification with the goals of education through increased involvement of parents.

> Plowden's concept of partnership with parents was underpinned by the notion of professionals exercising their specialist knowledge on behalf, and in support, of the best interests of children and their families ...
> It was not concerned with transferring power to parents.
> Professionals were disinterested, humanitarian and rational.
> (Armstrong 1995)

This view of professionals being objective and working first and foremost to meet the needs of the child is still current. For example some large LEAs have provision allocation meetings which examine assessments of need by professionals but do not include those professionals in that meeting in order to achieve some degree of objectivity. Many educational psychologists and SEN case workers will deny that often LEA decisions are subjective. They may deny valuing the efficient use of resources rather than the needs of the child.

In relation to special educational needs, Plowden went on to stress the important role of the parent, but that role was solely concerned with 'coming to terms' with their child's special needs.

> Teamwork is necessary between all concerned and, in this connection, we must stress the vital role of the parent ... they will be, at least, worried about it and they may feel acute distress,

3

bewilderment, resentment or even shame. They will almost certainly need help, first in accepting that their child is *not like other children* and then in understanding his needs ... all our evidence emphasises the need to advise and support the parents and to associate them as much as possible with the education of their child.

If it is necessary for a child to go to a special school, or still more, to a training centre, parents need to be helped to accept and understand the decision, and they should always be consulted well before it is made.

(CACE 1967, 843)

Remember this was thirty years ago. The key terms 'associate' and 'consult' would have been open to interpretation by the LEA, as are the newer terms that have replaced them.

Much progress has been made in recognising that while a child may have certain special educational needs which he or she shares with no other in the school, there are many common needs that the child shares with others in a school (e.g. Norwich 1996). These include the need to have success, to be part of a social group and to be respected as an individual.

The legacy of Warnock

The Warnock Report (DES 1978) on special educational needs set the scene for the 1981 Education Act and 'gave official legitimacy to the principal of parent–professional partnership in special education' (Armstrong 1996). However, in practice this was based on a model of involvement rather than partnership as there was no equal access to information. The term *disclosure* of information was used.

> We have insisted throughout this report that the successful education of children with special educational needs is dependent upon the full involvement of their parents: indeed, unless the parents are seen as equal partners in the educational process the purpose of our report will be frustrated.
>
> (DES 1978)

> Assessments should be seen as a partnership between teachers, other professionals and parents in a joint endeavour to discover and understand the nature of the difficulties and needs of individual children. Close relations should be established and maintained with parents and can only be helped by frankness and openness on all sides.
>
> (DES 1978)

In 1985 Warnock clarified what she meant:

> In educational matters, parents cannot be equals to teachers if teachers are to be regarded as professionals. Even though

4

educating a child is a joint enterprise involving both home and school, parents should realise that they cannot have the last word. *It is a question of collaboration not partnership.*

More positively the Warnock Report suggested that there was a need for a 'Named Person' to act as a knowledgeable but independent guide to parents seeking or being given a statement of special educational needs for their child. However, this was not included in the 1981 Education Act but it eventually found its way into the Code of Practice in 1994.

Warnock also weakened the link between the description of a child's needs and the location of consequent provision to meet those needs. The purpose of the statement did not have to be placement in one of a number of special schools each catering for a different cluster of needs. Thus there are decisions to be made as to what degree of provision is to be made and where that provision should be located.

It was no longer a case of:

Joan is maladjusted so she can go to the school for the maladjusted

    or

Mary has a severe hearing impairment so she should go to the school for the deaf

    or

Arthur is failing to thrive because of his asthma so he should go to school for the delicate and get some fresh air

    or

Poor Ronnie is a bit backward and just can't keep up so he would be better off at the school for children with moderate learning difficulties.

Mainstream schools began to respond to the challenge of including children with special needs and many LEAs started to adopt policies to support the integration of children with special needs.

The Warnock Report and the consequent 1981 Education Act had edged the door open to parental involvement in decision making at least in regard to statements. (It remains to be seen whether or not Warnock will find her place in history as a pioneer for parents' rights, ethics in embryology, one of the country's greatest philosophers or as Margaret Thatcher's bridesmaid.)

The 1988 Education Reform Act

This introduced the National Curriculum and gave schools strict requirements to teach and test across a specific range of subjects. Positively, it introduced the concept of entitlement for all children to a broad, balanced, relevant and differentiated curriculum which has often been a used as lever by parents since then. Broad and balanced meant that the curriculum should not be skewed to one area emphasising one subject to the detriment of others. Differentiation has been understood to mean different things to differing degrees by different schools and teachers. At its heart was the expectation that teachers should plan meaningful units of work that took into account the differing needs and backgrounds of their pupils. This could be facilitated by good parent–teacher partnership.

Testing across subjects naturally led to the establishment of league tables of schools through the publication of summary test scores.

Negatively, schools could opt out of LEA control and, if they could not openly select children, they could try their hardest not to take on potentially difficult children. Local Management of Schools (LMS) also meant that money was delegated to LEA schools on the basis of number of children on the school roll. Some governing bodies might perceive that pupils with special needs might be using 'more than their fair share' of the resources.

The Parents Charter was introduced which gave parents a choice of school *so long as there was space available for them.*

Paradoxically, the Educational Reform Act made parents into consumers of education through their right to choose but also made schools more selective consumers of their raw material, i.e. pupils.

The 1993 Act and Code of Practice

This responded to HMI and Audit Commission reports which highlighted concerns relating to special needs provision:
- that schools and local education authorities should be accountable for meeting special needs;
- LEA statements needed to be produced more quickly and be more specific;
- that special needs in mainstream schools should be addressed.

The 1993 Education Act did not significantly change the regulations of the 1981 Act, but included the establishment of SEN tribunals and published a Code of Practice on the Identification and Assessment of Special Educational Needs. It would have been helpful if its title had been 'Code of Practice on the Identification, Assessment and Provision for Special Educational Needs' since the document in its current form is not very forthcoming about provision. This may be due to the DFEE not wanting to be overly prescriptive to LEAs and parents, which if true, would be seen as ironic in light of concurrent moves towards government centralisation. More probably, it is an admission that children with special needs will get better or worse resources depending upon the area they live in. Actually, outlining the resources required to meet different needs would put the onus on the government to find the funds.

SEN tribunals

In order to deal with intractable disagreements between the LEA and parents about statements of special educational needs, an independent tribunal was set up as part of the 1993 Act. Tribunals are independent in that their members are appointed by the Secretaries of State for Education, but government cannot influence their decisions. The tribunal also does not have connections with any LEA.

The Code of Practice

This recognised a continuum of need with a consequential continuum of provision and proposed a staged approach. Special education provision can occur within residential special schools, special schools, special units within mainstream schools and in mainstream schools. Children with special educational needs have different degrees of difficulty which require different levels of support. Also a child's level of need may change as they develop during their school life so a flexible approach is suggested.

Principles

- special educational needs must be addressed;
- recognise a continuum of needs and provision;
- greatest possible access to a broad and balanced education;
- most children with SEN will be in mainstream with no statement and many children with a statement will also be in the mainstream;
- early intervention is important (LEA, health and social services);
- the partnership between parents and their children, schools, LEAs and other agencies.

The five stage model

Stage One: class or subject teachers identify or register a child's SEN and consulting the school's SENCO take initial action;

Stage Two: the school's SENCO takes the lead responsibility for gathering information and for coordinating the child's special education provision, working with the child's teachers;

Stage Three: teachers and the SENCO are supported by specialists from outside the school;

Stage Four: the LEA considers the need for a statutory assessment and makes a multidisciplinary assessment if appropriate;

Stage Five: the LEA considers the need for a statement of special educational needs and, if appropriate, makes a statement and arranges, monitors and reviews provision.

SEN tribunals

A parent can appeal to the tribunal if the LEA:
- refuses to make a formal assessment of their child's special educational needs;
- refuses to issue a statement of their child's special educational needs after making a formal assessment.

If the LEA have made a statement or have changed a previous statement, parents can appeal against:
- the description in the statement of their child's special educational needs;
- the description in the statement of special educational help that the LEA think the child should receive;
- the school named in the statement for their child to attend;
- the LEA not naming a school in the statement.

Parents can also appeal if the LEA:
- refuses to change the school named in the statement;
- refuses to reassess their child's special educational needs if they have not made a new assessment for at least six months;
- decides not to maintain a statement.

Parents cannot appeal to the tribunal against:
- the way the LEA carried out an assessment, or the length of time it took;
- the way the LEA are arranging to provide the help set out in their child's statement;
- the description in the statement of their child's non-educational needs or how the LEA plan to meet those needs.

 From Blamires, M., Robertson, C. and Blamires, J. (1997) *Parent–Teacher Partnership*. London: David Fulton Publishers.

The first three stages are referred to as the 'school-based stages' as this is where the school will be taking the lead in ensuring provision is being made. Stages Four and Five are concerned with the consideration of the allocation of a statement of special educational need and responsibility lies with the LEA.

A set of 'triggers' or decisions govern the entry and consequent movement through these stages. As one might expect these are, potentially, a great source of disagreement between parents and professionals. Indeed, the fact that a school has decided that a child should be put on the special needs register can be devastating for parents and needs more sensitive handling than just a 'letter home'.

The Code of Practice itself is clearly written with a 'Crystal Clear' mark from the plain English campaign. It is also available at the cost of a telephone call and is therefore a welcome document for parents and teachers alike. Be aware of alternative 'idiot guides' which interpret the code according to the personal priorities of the author.

Parents now have more rights to involvement in meeting their child's special educational needs, yet these rights are being undermined by three elements of current educational legislation.

League tables

These are published summaries of GCSE results and take little or no account of the amount of progress a child has made in the school or the abilities of the children when they enter the school. League tables do not measure a school's success with children with special educational needs and until they do schools will concentrate on helping the children who do count within the league.

Local management and opting out of LEA control

This means that schools are less under the influence of the LEA and local community. Special needs provision may become less of a priority within schools and they may be reluctant to host new or existing specialist units of provision, e.g. for speech and language impairment or emotional/behavioural difficulty, as these units are seen to 'go against the desired image of a successful school'.

Increasing selection

This does not favour children with special educational needs as they can be perceived as being more difficult and 'a drain on limited resources'. In the context of league tables, success with children with special educational needs usually 'just does not count'.

Summary: the triple whammy against thirty years of evolving practice and experience

9

There is a danger that the partnership between parents, school and community is under threat with a move towards the increasing isolation of parents of children with special needs as obtaining provision becomes an individual's legal negotiation with the LEA and an increasingly reluctant school.

Chapter 2

Why Parent–Teacher Partnership is Important

Legislation has allocated increasing rights to parents and children over recent years which culminate in their increased involvement in decision-making processes. This makes demands on even the most literate of parents in negotiating and securing appropriate provision for their child. That mainly 'confident middle-class' families appear to be more successful in navigating the systems should be considered an indictment of the systems in place at the moment, rather than these parents or the principles underlying these processes.

The legal view

You as a parent, have a right to take part in decisions about your child's education and to be kept in touch at all stages. Your views are very important.... If you have any worries at any time, make sure you share them with your child's teacher, or one of the professionals working with your child as well as one of your friends or family.

(DFEE 1994b)

The rights of parents

Remember that you know your child better than any one. The closer you work with your child's teacher and school, the more successful any special help will be.

(DFEE 1994b)

The above extracts from the DFEE parents' booklet on special educational needs clearly stress not only the importance of the parents' role in providing information about any concerns about a child's development, but also that their active educational and motivational involvement is vital.

The tribunal

The existence of the tribunal as outlined above further stresses the active role that parents can have within the decision-making procedures on needs and educational provision when a statement is being considered by an LEA for a child.

The OFSTED view

The OFSTED handbook on inspection requires inspectors to evaluate and report on the following aspects of a school's partnership with parents:

> The effectiveness of the school's partnership with parents, highlighting strengths and weaknesses in terms of:
> (i) the information provided about the school, and about pupils' work and progress through annual and other reports and parents' meetings;
> (ii) parents' involvement with the school and with their children's work at home;
> Judgements should be based on the extent to which links with parents contribute to pupils' learning.
>
> (OFSTED 1995a)

This refers to all parents and can be seen to be the basis from which a school's partnership with parents of children with special needs can be developed.

The handbook goes on to stress:

> Overall judgements need to establish whether:
> there are clear lines of communication;
> the school's approach to relations with parents is maintained consistently;
> the school does all it can to gain the involvement of all parents.
>
> (OFSTED 1995a)

In order to gain this evidence a questionnaire is sent out to all parents and a pre-inspection meeting for parents is held which does not involve representatives of the school other than to introduce the inspector or inspectors who will run the meeting. Staff who have children at the school can attend this meeting. Inspectors may also gather evidence from documentation, information provided to parents, discussion with parent helpers and home–school diaries.

Specifically, in relation to special educational needs, the inspectors will examine the extent of parent involvement in annual reviews of statements and in Individual Educational Plans. In addition the inspectors will seek out to what extent the school's policy on special educational needs is operating effectively; that the governing body of the school reports to parents annually on the success of this policy and any changes in it; and the effectiveness of the allocation of resources over the previous year to pupils with special educational needs and any consultation with the LEA, funding authority or other schools. Parents of children with special educational needs should also know who their main point of contact is (normally the SENCO) and who is the school's 'responsible person'. (This is usually the headteacher or member of the school's governing body who is ultimately responsible for special needs provision in the school.)

From an examination of OFSTED reports, schools have been praised on their partnership with parents when:
- parents have reported receiving quick responses to requests;
- parents have received a regular newsletter with a forthcoming diary of events;
- a member of staff or a working group has been given responsibility for developing home–school liaison;
- information on children's progress is clearly presented to parents with opportunities for follow-up discussion;
- there is good use of home–school contact methods such as diaries and logs;
- there is development of parental involvement in teaching their child through lending libraries for books/games or toys.

It would be wrong to assume that the impact of OFSTED inspections is always a positive one with regard to special educational needs and parental involvement. As Wragg and Brighouse (1995) have noted, the system of inspection currently deployed tends to operate on a 'hit and run' basis and is not necessarily going to contribute to school improvement. It will not, in all probability bring about improvements in SEN provision that are sustainable and meaningful to either parents or school staff. This is because it is quite clearly detached from advice or support.

So, schools and parents should not expect OFSTED inspection to serve as a major vehicle for improving SEN provision and parental partnership. However, inspection might usefully highlight focus points for action, and therefore be a positive catalyst for change and development.

Self-evaluation of SEN policy and provision, and of associated partnership with parents is likely to bring about more meaningful and lasting improvement than the visitation of OFSTED. This does not mean that schools and parents should simply continue working in *ad hoc* ways with each other, following traditional practices and accepting 'norms' that parents and staff have concerns about. Development of good practice should, if it is to be really beneficial, stem from the interests of various interested parties, who devise better practice together. The now defunct School Curriculum Development Committee (SCDC) produced some good resource materials in the 1980s called GRIDS (Guidelines for Review and Internal Development in Schools) to help schools develop as educational communities. In the GRIDS publications (e.g. 1988, 1989) a structured approach is advocated to the reviewing of various aspects of SEN provision, and to the reviewing of parental partnership. Of particular note, is the way that the material specifically seeks parental perspectives on school development.

The school's view

Requirements for the extent of partnership between schools and parents are outlined below in the DFEE circular sent to all schools and LEAs:

> The school's policy should contain a clear statement of the school's arrangements for ensuring close working partnership with parents of children with special educational needs. Those arrangements should be drawn up having regard to the Code of Practice.... and which cover such matters as involving parents when a concern is first expressed within the school, arrangements for incorporating parents' views in assessment and subsequent reviews; and arrangements for ensuring that parents are fully informed about the school's procedures and are made welcome in the school.
>
> (DFEE Circular 6/94, para. 52)

The LEA view

The LEA plays the central role in issuing a statement of special needs. If the parents' knowledge is to be taken into account and their views included, then a partnership has to develop between the LEA and the parents.

> If parents are advised and supported from the start there should be fewer anxieties and disagreements about the proposed statement, if issued, and a stronger bond of agreement about the best way for the child....
>
> LEAs should encourage parents to seek the help of their Named Person in preparing their advice and should welcome the Named Person at any meetings.
>
> LEAs should work closely with local parent or other voluntary organisations in order to develop partnership and support systems and information material on which parents may draw when assessments are being made.
>
> (DFEE 1994a, 3:102)

The Named Person is someone who is, ideally, independent of the LEA who can assist parents of children undergoing statutory assessment. They may be a friend, neighbour or relative, a representative from a parents' group or voluntary organisation or a professional who is not contributing to a particular child's assessment.

Local support groups run by parents for parents have an important role to play here as have DFEE-funded LEA parent–partnership schemes in providing advice and support to parents and training Named Persons.

While the Named Person is important and their role is discussed later in this book, the Named Officer's responsibilities should not be understated. They have an important role in ensuring that parents get the right information in the appropriate format to begin with. To this end in some authorities they work with local parents groups to produce 'Induction Packs' to introduce the parents to the process and host 'surgeries' for parents and Named Persons to ensure everyone understands the process of statutory assessment.

The Named Person

The LEA must identify a Named Person when sending parents a final statement.

The Named Person:
- may be appointed at the start of the assessment process;
- should be appointed in cooperation with parents;
- should be independent of the LEA, e.g. from a voluntary organisation or parent partnership scheme;
- can give parents information and advice.

The Named LEA Officer

LEAs must identify the named LEA officer when sending parents a proposal to make a statutory assessment. This officer:
- acts as a source of information for parents within the LEA;
- liaises with parents on arrangements relating to statutory assessment and the statement.

Chapter 3

Barriers to Partnership: From the Other Side of the Fence

Parents are individuals, they do not necessarily have anything in common except the fact that they have children. They cannot be lumped together as a group who all need to be 'dealt with' in the same way and it cannot be assumed that there are magic answers or tricks or formulae to use to ensure smooth and effective partnership with them. Attempts to subdivide parents, to fit them into various categories and apply the appropriate solution will result in an ever expanding number of categories and an equal number of different solutions.

Parents of children with special educational needs do sometimes have experiences in common and often have concerns in common. It may be helpful to bear these in mind always in parallel with the important understanding that all parents are different. In trying to build a partnership professionals should avoid generalisations and wrong assumptions so that parents are not made to feel that they are expected to fit a stereotype.

Parents are emotionally involved with their children in a way that professionals, however caring, are not. This is the one great difference between parents and teachers and one that needs to be acknowledged at the outset and kept in mind throughout the partnership. 'I understand exactly how you feel' is *always* the wrong thing to say. It can never be true in any situation and can feel patronising to parents who do not wish to have their complex feelings dismissed by such easy understanding.

It is simplistic to suggest that parents will go through a well-defined 'grieving process' beginning by becoming aware of their child's special needs and coming out at the other end of the process accepting the difficulty and adjusted to the new path their life will take. For parents of children with special needs there is often no clear path, expectations and assumptions have to be constantly revised,

Emotional barriers

17

there is shock, bewilderment, isolation and sadness and anger and at the same time there is often pressure (self-imposed or from outside) to take action, to make decisions and to 'deal with' the situation.

The strong and complex emotions described above can lead to practical problems and create extra hurdles to be jumped on the way to achieving worthwhile partnership.

Isolation

Parents of children with special needs can experience a sense of isolation in many different forms, some obvious, some subtle, some physical and some less concrete.

Mothers and fathers

It is often assumed that when two parents are involved with their child's education they speak with one voice and present a united front. That assumption is certainly made in the Code of Practice and in the procedures surrounding statutory assessment. It is acknowledged that when parents are divorced or separated the situation may not be so clear but there is seldom any recognition of the fact that two people faced with what may be the most life-changing, emotionally demanding events of their lives as parents may not react in unison and may not have identical perceptions of the problem or its solution.

Mothers and fathers do not usually have the same experience of or with their child. One may see their child with his/her peer group much more frequently and be able to make comparisons about development and progress, one parent may attend many more clinic appointments or assessments with the child and hear the advice and opinion of the professionals concerned at first hand. The other may only receive relayed information and see written reports but not the assessments that led to those reports. Parents may have differing expectations and hopes for their child. The shock of a diagnosis or realisation that something is wrong may lead to a period of denial or depression and an inability to discuss the situation with someone else who is also in a state of grief or shock. There may be a sense of guilt or shame which prevents open communication. As mentioned elsewhere, parents may work towards an understanding and acceptance of their child's special need at different rates and whereas it is *acceptable* for professionals to differ in their *professional* view of a child's problems, it is generally expected that parents will be in agreement. This can put a great strain on parents, firstly, because they feel there is an expectation that they will agree, secondly, because they may find it hard to come to any decision when one of them is not in favour and thirdly, because they may feel isolated and unsupported by the person they expect to be closest to.

The wider family

Despite the much lamented breakdown of the extended family, children do not exist in isolation with their parents. There may be siblings, aunts, uncles and cousins, not forgetting grandparents, all forming part of the whole family jigsaw puzzle. Each of these family members will have their own hopes and expectations for their wider family. For the parents of a child with special needs the wider family may become yet another problem rather than the supportive group they need. Further removed from the child than its parents, relatives may not see or may not wish to see the reality of the problems. Attempts to say the 'right' thing, for example, 'she'll grow out of it' or 'you were just the same at his age' may seem to be denials of the difficulties. Grandparents expecting a rewarding relationship with their grandchildren with none of the worry of being totally responsible may be unsure of their role. The child's parents may feel they have failed to produce what was expected. It is not easy to continually point out real difficulties to grandparents anxious to dote over 'perfect' grandchildren and it is not easy to decide how open to be about difficulties that may only worry relatives who will then feel powerless to help. Even with the most aware and helpful relatives there can be differences in perspective. Choices about education can be even harder to make when other (possibly less well informed or simply outdated) views are taken into consideration.

Friends

Many of the quandaries faced by family members may also apply to friends. They may feel guilty about having children without special needs. They may not know how to broach the subject of a child who is different or how much to talk about the problems they have with their own 'ordinary' children without seeming to be insensitive. This ultra-sensitivity may lead to more feelings of isolation for the parents of the disabled child, but at the same time they may well feel occasional resentment at the apparently easy lives their friends are able to lead.

There are no easy answers or lists of rules of behaviour for relatives and friends, but it is probably fair to say that a clumsy expression of concern or an awkwardly phrased enquiry about a child's progress is preferable to no mention of the problem at all. Relatives and friends cannot be expected to *know* how parents are feeling but they can make the effort to *ask*. They may not know the best way to help but they can still offer to help.

However overwhelming the problems may sometimes seem, parents still want to be seen as people first. Parents frequently stress their wish to be treated as a 'normal' family. This does not mean they continually wish away the child's special needs, but it may mean that they want to be recognised as individuals with personalities, interests, likes and dislikes that are not all defined by the special needs of their child or their role as its parents.

The wider community from the playground outwards

The primary school playground at the beginning and end of the day can be a competitive arena, a minefield of sensitivities and a very lonely place for a parent of a child with special needs.

If a child attends a special school with transport provided, the school gate culture with its possible network of support from other parents does not exist at all. The parents who have most need of contact and reassurance from each other have least exposure to other parents. This lack of contact can be counteracted to some extent by the formation of parent-led but school-facilitated support groups. Travel and accessibility are still likely to be barriers to communication between parents, but school communications should try to demonstrate avenues for obtaining information and support from other parents so that, even if they are not actively used, parents can be reassured that they are not alone.

In mainstream schools, access to support from other parents of children with special needs may seem even more difficult. Schools do not tend to advertise their systems for meeting special needs in the same way as they display their successes in test results and league tables. There can seem to be a conspiracy of silence when it comes to discussing special needs provision which means that, at best, information is distributed on a 'need to know' basis to those parents whose children have been identified as having special needs. Parents may have no idea of how to access the system if they are worried about their child's progress. Parents who are aware of their own child's needs and provision may have no idea of how many other children in the school have special needs and certainly no way of identifying their parents. Playground chat may extend to a comparison of which reading book one's child is on, but not to which stage of the Code of Practice a child is on.

Schools which describe their special needs provision at the outset to all parents and who offer follow-up information and discussion to parents of children with special needs *as a group as well as individually* can help to decrease the sense of isolation felt by parents.

The 'system'

As suggested above, it is sometimes a lack of information about what is happening or what should be happening that creates a barrier to partnership. The Code of Practice provides a detailed framework but it is not easy reading at first sight and is not easily assimilated. It is also, necessarily, open to interpretation by each school and LEA so that while its principles must be adhered to it does not seek to prescribe what should happen in the classroom. Even the most literate and well-informed parent might have difficulty relating the guidelines in the Code of Practice to what happens to their own child, particularly in the first three, non-statutory assessment stages.

The staged approach, the IEP and the system of review are all welcome as agreed frameworks for action, but they and the process of formal assessment are all very much 'paper led'. It has been said that in order to cope with the special needs system you need to be the sort of person who keeps all their receipts. Parents who find paperwork difficult to deal with at the best of times may feel overwhelmed, parents who have no problems with day-to-day paperwork may feel overwhelmed when the papers relate to their child and its problems. The language used ('statementing' smacks of certification) and the procedures involved (signing an agreement to one's child being assessed can feel like signing the child and your hopes for it away) are legalistic and the background knowledge needed to play a full part in the process can be daunting. At the same time the parents are put in a position of great responsibility, for example, when the proposed statement is issued only the *parents* have the right to appeal against it.

Teachers and schools should not feel that they are expected to have all the answers. It can be helpful for parents to be put in touch with national and local support and information groups.

'Superparent'

A parent of a child with special needs can be made to feel inadequate if they are not able to be the 'perfect partner' with the school or LEA. As well as all the barriers mentioned above there may be other reasons why parents feel inadequate.

Unreasonable expectations from the school

'Now that your child has been moved to Stage Two that means you must do extra spelling practice with him at home' (even though it is almost impossible to get him to complete his homework, eat his tea, stop hitting his little brother, come home before midnight).

'We know you parents are the experts so you tell us what would be best for him' (even though you have already tried the contradictory advice of every expert you have met and the magic solution has not appeared).

Despair

Parents can sometimes reach a stage where they feel there is no point discussing things any more. They may be tired of continually explaining and describing their child's difficulties (usually from conception onwards) and lose faith in the stream of professionals who listen, take notes and move on. There may seem to be nothing to be gained from continued talking when no one is going to be able to solve the problem and they will be left to cope in the end anyway.

Fear

Parents may fear the consequences of acknowledging their worries. They may feel they are seen as a nuisance, they may feel their comments will be seen as criticism of the school, they may fear that their child will be moved to a different school or ostracised.

Exhaustion

It is often physically and almost always mentally exhausting to look after a child with special needs. Parents may never get a proper night's sleep, they may never have time to themselves, they may feel they are expected to do more because their child needs them more. It is not always easy to get a babysitter for a child who needs special care. There may not be a network of friends from the child's peer group to create a social life for the child and a consequent break for the parents. The child may need to be lifted, pushed in a wheelchair, exercised and fed. There may be no time or energy left to sit back and look at the whole picture and think calmly about what the next steps should be.

Indifference

I include this heading only to be able to dismiss it. Parents may shy away from contact with schools and professionals for all sorts of reasons but there are very few if any genuinely indifferent parents. We may all be guilty of delaying a visit to the dentist but that is not because we are indifferent as to whether we have toothache or not.

To go back to the beginning of this chapter, parents are individuals. They need to be consulted, to be kept informed and to be treated with respect. The onus is on the professionals to use all the strategies at their disposal to help parents to feel included and that everyone is on the same side of the fence.

Meetings

For parents almost any meeting about their child feels like a crisis meeting. Whenever their child's difficulties are discussed memories of the initial (gradual or sudden) realisation of the child's difficulty may be aroused and the implications for the child's future will be brought to mind. One of the greatest worries for parents is what will happen when their child leaves school; a reception class teacher does not need to look so far ahead but needs to be aware that parents may be doing so.

Parents will deal with their emotions in a variety of ways but they cannot be expected to be unaffected by them. Bursting into tears, losing one's temper or being super-efficient may all be signs of the same underlying sadness or confusion. However, it would be dangerous to draw conclusions from these outward expressions of emotion. They do *not* mean that the parent cannot cope, is being unrealistic in their expectations or has failed to come to terms with their child's problems. Because a meeting is stressful for a parent it does not mean that they would prefer not to have a meeting. Part of the reason for the high level of stress experienced by parents may be that the meeting *is* important.

People do not find strong emotions easy to deal with. Parents may avoid asking questions they want to ask or discussing aspects of their child they would like to discuss because they are afraid of being embarrassed by breaking down or becoming angry; teachers may worry about upsetting parents and feel that they have caused the emotional upset by the way they have talked about the child.

Meetings that are calm and business-like, that are unhurried, that have a clear agenda where appropriate, that are seen as part of a continuing pattern of further meetings and not as one-off decision times and where the child's abilities and difficulties are discussed honestly and openly but positively, should be able to achieve what they set out to achieve regardless of the emotional roller-coaster they may seem to all involved.

Some steps towards productive meetings with parents:

- if a 'professionals only' meeting is necessary before or after the meeting with parents tell the parents about this. At the same time avoid showing parents into a room full of professionals who have apparently just finished discussing them. If possible make sure parents enter the room first and leave last;
- have a clear, written agenda, however brief which also states who will be at the meeting. Make sure parents receive this well before the day of the meeting;
- at the start of the meeting introduce everybody, explain their role, avoid jargon and avoid 'chumminess' between professionals. Make the parent feel included not excluded;
- encourage parents to bring a friend or supporter to the meeting;
- encourage the parents or supporter to make notes if they want to;
- make sure minutes are taken and distributed promptly;
- make it clear at the outset how long has been allowed for the meeting and that a further meeting will be arranged if necessary;
- allow time at the end of the meeting to make sure both parents have had an opportunity to say all they wanted to say and to ask all the questions they wanted to ask.

Some children with special educational needs may have some form of long-term disability. It may be physical, sensory or medical in nature, for example, cerebral palsy, visual impairment or epilepsy. It may be difficult for teachers to 'come to terms' with a child's disability. They may think of the child as a condition rather than an individual or make unrealistic demands upon the child due to ignorance.

Information from the SENCO, specialist advisory teacher or local or national source of expertise can help the teacher to understand the educational implications of the condition. Information on how it affects the individual and how the individual reacts to the condition can be best obtained from the parents. They may also have tried and tested management strategies.

A barrier to partnership may occur when parents may not accept that their child has a disability or the extent of the disability. In some cases this refusal to 'come to terms' has had positive outcomes. It has

'Coming to terms'

23

meant that some parents have regained control from professionals who have proposed unduly pessimistic futures for their children. Parents of children with Down's syndrome in the 1960s and 1970s such as Rex Brinkworth refused to 'come to terms' and sought extra and appropriate provision for their children so that now many children with Down's syndrome are educated in mainstream schools.

The following account by Emily Pearl, who explains what it is like to have a child with a disability, is moving and eloquent and is a strong example of how parents may feel. We all have hopes and dreams for our children. The birth of a child who may not fulfil these dreams but be a possible concern for the rest of their lives requires an adjustment which may take years or may never occur. Many parents may not be able explain their frustrations and sense of grief as well as Emily Pearl. This is a powerful description which can help others to understand a little of what it is like.

Hornby (1995) lists the challenges that parents of children with a disability must overcome in just coping from day to day. It is a pretty awesome job description which few people would want in addition to the normal life stresses that families have to deal with anyway.

If the child has two parents one of them may be further down this list than the other so it cannot be guaranteed that a professional has common agreement with parents just because they have talked to one of them. Frequently, it is the mother who is further on in accepting the challenges that have to be faced because she tends to more involved with the child on a day-to-day basis. However, in a society with many different work patterns and lifestyles as well as different people, this cannot always be assumed.

Parents may like to be put in touch with other parents of children with similar difficulties through local parent support groups. It may help the school if a representative from such a group visits the school to talk with staff on a development day or evening.

LEA restraints

In one sense the Code of Practice had an advantage for a penny-pinching LEA in that it sets another set of hurdles for schools to surmount before they can attempt to obtain a statement.

The LEA's budget for special educational needs is part of the whole budget for education. The LEA does not get extra money from the government for every statement it issues. Therefore the more it spends on statements the less there is for the other parts of the education budget. It has the choice of making lots of statements each with limited funding or fewer statements that have larger funding.

A number of authorities such as Hampshire, Kent and Tower Hamlets have implemented auditing procedures to establish clear criteria for different levels of funding up to and including statements. In this context the Code of Practice can be seen as validating such an approach.

Welcome to Holland

By Emily Pearl

I am often asked to describe the experience of raising a child with a disability – to try to help people who have not shared that unique experience to understand it, to imagine how it would feel.

It's like this …

When you're going to have a baby it's like planning a fabulous vacation trip – to Italy. You buy a bunch of guide books and make your wonderful plans. The coliseum, the Michelangelo David, the gondolas in Venice. You may learn some handy phrases in Italian. It's all very exciting. After months of eager anticipation the day finally arrives. You pack your bags and off you go. Several hours later the plane lands. The stewardess comes in and says, 'Welcome to Holland'.

'Holland!?!' you say. 'What do you mean, Holland? I signed up for Italy! I'm supposed to be in Italy! All my life I've dreamed of going to Italy.'

But there's been a change of flight plan. You've landed in Holland and there you must stay.

The important thing is that they haven't taken you to a horrible, disgusting place full of pestilence, famine and disease. It's just a different place. So you must go out and buy new guide books. And you will learn a whole new language. And you will meet a whole new group of people you never would have met.

It's just a different place. It's slower paced than Italy, less flashy than Italy. But after you have been there for a while and you catch your breath you look around and you begin to notice that Holland has tulips, Holland even has Rembrandts.

But everyone you know is busy coming and going from Italy and they're all bragging about what a wonderful time they had there. And for the rest of your life you will say, 'Yes, that's where I was supposed to go. That's what I had planned.'

And the pain of that will never ever go away, because the loss of that dream is a significant loss.

But if you spend your whole life mourning the fact that you didn't get to Italy, you may never be free to enjoy the very special, the very lovely things about Holland.

> Under the 1993 Education Act, the LEA must respond to a request for a statement within a strict time scale.
>
> Assessment and statement: the timetable
> - Considering whether a statutory assessment is necessary 6 weeks
> - Making the assessment 10 weeks
> - Drafting the proposed statement or note in lieu 2 weeks
> - Finalising the statement 8 weeks
> - Total 26 weeks
>
> (SEN regulations set out exceptions to time limits)

This may mean that they have to take short cuts. Some LEA representatives believe that this introduces a conveyor belt approach which will be detrimental to the LEA's partnership with parents in identifying needs and suitable provision (e.g. Dyer 1995). In some cases LEAs have started to use banks of phrases on computer describing needs and consequent provision to produce quick 'off the peg' statements. One can sympathise with their reasons for this short cut but it is at the cost of individually tailored provision.

Non-educational provision

The LEA may have difficulty in negotiating and obtaining provision from health or social services as part of a statement even when roles are clearly mapped out within the Code of Practice, as it may not be given a high priority within that service because it is viewed as educational legislation.

Access to speech and language therapy has always been a bugbear in this area because therapists are employed by the health service which sets them a wider brief than 'just' education.

In the case of health it is also quite difficult to gain access to the members of the quango controlling a local Health Trust in comparison to elected members of LEA educational committees.

None the less a number of innovative schemes have been put in place through joint funding between health and education *in some areas*. This includes the funding of communication aids and the allocation of speech and language therapy within mainstream schools.

Why do some parents not want to participate in their child's education?

The false allocation of blame and guilt

Some parents may feel guilty about their child's special educational needs and communication from the school may be interpreted as criticism. They may feel they are being blamed for their child's difficulties and this can lead to resentment towards the school. This in turn may be perceived by the school as a lack of interest in the school's efforts or even hostility. The Code of Practice recognises the

From guilt to animosity

Guilt is one of the most fundamental and persistent reactions that parents – particularly mothers – experience. Once the habit of guilt has formed, it is very difficult to break. Everything becomes 'their fault'; a real persecution complex can develop easily.

The slightest criticism or negative observation is taken as a personal criticism, for which blame must be acknowledged.

(Gascoigne 1995)

Comment	Interpretation
• 'He doesn't do his homework'	• 'I am not helping him enough with his homework'
• 'She won't ask for help'	• 'I've brought her up to be too independent'
• 'He doesn't seem to know how to play with other children'	• 'I should have taken him to more playgroups'
• 'She has not developed pre-reading skills'	• 'I should have spent more time reading with her'
• 'He's very keen on Postman Pat, isn't he?'	• 'I let him watch too much television'

From Blamires, M., Robertson, C. and Blamires, J. (1997) *Parent–Teacher Partnership*. London: David Fulton Publishers.

initial problem of perceived blame but could hinder a developing partnership by stressing recognition of parental responsibilities.

Other parents may not be ready to take on board the full implications of their responsibilities for their child's special educational needs for reasons outlined below or because they 'have not yet come to terms' with their child's special needs.

> Parents may feel that they are being blamed for their child's difficulties when the school first raises questions with them. Nonetheless, schools should make every effort to encourage parents to recognise that they have responsibilities to their child, and that the most effective provision will be made when they are open and confident in working in partnership with the school and professionals.
>
> (DFEE 1994a, 2:29)

Alienation from the aims for education – a negative cycle of expectations

Many parents may not identify with the aims of the school for a variety of reasons. They may find it difficult to communicate their views effectively or cooperate with the school to meet their child's needs. Some teachers adopt a formal manner which they believe is in keeping with their professional status when dealing with parents. This may be perceived as cold and distant by parents who may be worried about coming into school anyway.

Moses and Croll (1985) note that teachers have a number of explanations of children's difficulties which place a heavy emphasis on the social circumstances and parental background, but fail to recognise the role that the school or teaching may play. They suggest that such views will hardly be firm foundations for an effective partnership. It may be even worse now in that more simplistic explanations for a child's difficulties are being encouraged, for example, the *Sun* newspaper headline of 1996, 'Is this the worst behaved child in Britain?'

Parents may feel that they do not have time or the skills to help their child at home. They may also find it difficult to get into school to attend meetings because of childcare problems or working patterns.

Having a child with any special educational need may cause extra stress and worry as well as imposing additional responsibilities on the parent.

A newly qualified teacher on an autism course complained that, 'parental involvement was all well and good but what if the parent wouldn't do what she was told?' The teacher had set targets for the child to achieve at home with her parent but they were rarely carried out. When asked about home circumstances the teacher reported that the parent had two other preschool children as well as her eldest child with autism and was a single parent.

That the parent was coping wasn't recognised as a success in itself and without support from the community it was not realistic to set those targets.

As a parent said to the head of a school for children with moderate learning difficulties, *'Education is your area, I have enough on my plate!'*

What can a school do in the face of such negativity? Parents need:
- to know that they are needed;
- to know that what they say is being listened to and acted upon;
- to share in the successes of their children not just their failures.

This can be a barrier because some schools may have large numbers of children with special educational needs. For example some schools have 40 per cent or more children with special needs compared to the notional national average of 20 per cent. This can pose quite a problem for administration if time is not allocated for parental consultation and appropriate administrative IT systems are not in place.

By having whole-school systems for communication with parents, the requirements for parental involvement to meet special educational needs can be shared.

Time management in schools

Parents who are worried about their children are keen if not desperate to find an explanation. Periodically the media produces stories and articles about different syndromes and conditions which have an educational effect, for example dyslexia, Asperger syndrome, ME, or ADD/ADHD. Is it surprising that parents will want to investigate these labels as possible explanations? Teachers may also want to consider the needs of a child who is causing concern in terms of these labels.

The problem is that these labels can be a bit sticky so that both professionals and parents can get stuck in their thinking. The child becomes stereotyped by the label and the child's individual needs are overtaken by the received wisdom pertaining to the condition. The label becomes an end point rather than a signpost to further understanding.

Labels can help a parent to make a case for their child's needs. That he is not being lazy or naughty or just 'a bit disorganised'. The label can help to make the school reassess or take seriously the concerns of the parent and may help in obtaining resources and support.

Resource/role conflicts: the clash of labels

Where do labels lead?

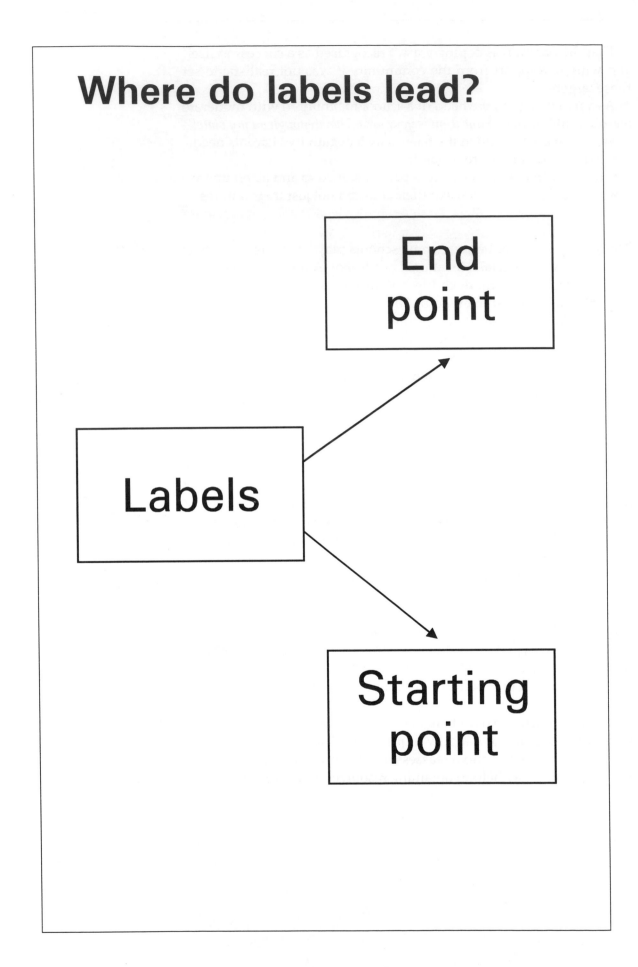

End point

Labels

Starting point

From Blamires, M., Robertson, C. and Blamires, J. (1997) *Parent–Teacher Partnership*. London: David Fulton Publishers.

Educational psychologists employed by LEAs are sometimes very reluctant to use labels because the labels carry a lot of baggage and to use them may imply the acceptance of a set of almost implicit assumptions about provision which they would be loath to surrender to. To use Hornby's model, they are, after all, the experts on education and not the parents or the label's lobby group.

A new pseudo social science appears to have emerged among some writers considering parental partnership. Its key writers haven't given it a name yet but it might be described as 'parentology' and be concerned with the classification of parents of children with special needs.

Types of parent?

> There are distinct groupings of parents who have common patterns when they deal with professionals. How they appear and behave does not necessarily correspond with how they feel inside. If professionals only respond to them according to how they appear, the risk of partnership breaking down are high.
>
> (Gascoigne 1995)

If you are not a parent of a child with special needs consider this:
- if you did have a child with such difficulties which group would you like to lumped into?
- to what extent can mutual respect be fostered while these groupings are actively advocated?

Surely, parents are people too and not just crude stereotypes? Yet again labels may be creating barriers to partnership. It wouldn't be acceptable to publish similar descriptions of education professionals or would it – the anxious teacher, the angry teacher, the tired teacher, the emotionally detached educational psychologist, the fighting SENCO?

More positively Jean Gross (1996) has suggested that there are two types of parents of children with special educational needs:
- involved articulate parents who want information often before they have to ask for it, need to feel genuinely heard and to be assured that any extra provision is being reliably undertaken. They may also want to do something to help the situation;
- reluctant parents who do not feel confident about their rights or about coming into school, who need to be talked to appropriately, stressing positive achievements alongside difficulties and with whom care should be taken not to attribute blame.

31

Types of parent

On the basis of her own experience Gascoigne gives us seven types of parent to consider: which one are you or which one do you encounter the most of?

Articulate, assertive, educated parents	'Appear to understand what they are talking about', 'without the complication of their child's special needs, teachers would prefer to deal with this type of parent'	'Inside they may be bewildered with feelings of inadequacy and helplessness', 'they may not know as much as they let on they know'
Angry, knowledgeable parents	'Well informed yet unable to be calm in discussion, view professionals with some contempt', 'may quote chapter and verse from Acts'	'Inside, they may have little regard for the expertise available to them or the constraints that professionals work under'
Acquiescent or submissive parents	'These parents will agree to almost anything a professional suggests'	'These parents do not have the confidence in their own status as expert on their own child' 'They will not complain'
Uncaring parents	'Some parents appear unconcerned that their child is falling behind ... and have low expectations from life generally'	'Many are simply afraid of the educational system and have had poor educational experiences themselves'
Angry, ill-informed parents	'Behave in a confrontational manner', 'harangue professionals over the phone, will not listen to reason'	'These parents care deeply and desperately about their children but are confused about educational systems'
Fighting parents	'More interested in the fight than the result, seem to take delight pursuing the argument and scoring points and lose sight of the immediate goals for their child'	'Their main aim is to battle with the gate keeper, do not realise that everyone is pursuing the same objective'
Special needs parents	In many ways all parents of children with special needs are themselves special needs parents. The emotional psychological baggage most parents carry with them can handicap them in approaching the whole process, but there is a specific group who may have difficulties in communicating their views and knowledge because they themselves have special needs.'	'These parents may be frustrated, patronised and marginalised because their views are not being heard or responded to.'

 From Blamires, M., Robertson, C. and Blamires, J. (1997) *Parent–Teacher Partnership*. London: David Fulton Publishers.

As parent–teacher partnership has evolved it has involved the parent more actively. The following description may help in considering where partnership broadly is with your school or LEA.

Types of parental partnership

Passive recipient of expertise

Professionals:
- regard themselves as the experts on all aspects of the functioning of children with special needs and parents' views are accorded little credence;
- maintain control over decisions while the parents' role is to receive information and instructions from professionals about their children with special needs;
- encourage the parent to be submissive and dependent;
- may ignore or overlook important knowledge that the parents have or the difficulties they face.

A source of information for professionals

This was the form of partnership envisaged by Warnock as described above. Parents provide valuable if not unique information for the professionals who can then decide upon the appropriate course of action in 'the best interests of the child' and making 'the best use of available resources'.

Wolfendale (1992) suggests that parents can make an invaluable contribution to assessment of a child's needs for the following reasons:
- parents are able to make realistic appraisals of their children;
- parents have extensive knowledge of their children's development from birth onwards;
- parents have intimate knowledge of the family circumstances which affect the child;
- parents have knowledge of other factors related to the wider social environment in which the family lives which have an impact on the child;
- parents can supply knowledge of children's behaviour in the home setting which may well be different from that at school;
- information from parents complements that from professionals and can therefore serve to highlight concerns regarding progress.

At its extreme this is a medical model not too dissimilar to the Triage system employed in accident and emergency units to decide who is the most urgent case. Parents are passive providers of information. The professionals then go off and 'do what they have to do'. It may be not surprising then that parents may perceive that they have little control of events within this form of partnership.

More positively, actively seeking this information from parents can be the first stage of a developing partnership for a school because it can:
- inform differentiation, tailoring curriculum areas to individual interests as well as responding to different cultural values;
- help overcome negative attitudes or attributions of cause held by staff.

Parents as consumers of provision

Parents:
- are regarded as consumers of professional services. The professional acts as a consultant, while the parents decide what action is to be taken;
- have control over the decision-making process, while professionals provide them with relevant information and a range of options to choose from;
- are more likely to be satisfied with the service they receive, but Hornby (1995) suggests it can lead to an abdication of responsibility by the professional where decisions are not made in the best interests of the child or within the constraints for *efficient use of resources*;
- usually want to know, when presented with this model, whether any LEA provision has been seriously implemented to any realistic degree.

Parents as a resource to be managed

Within this model professionals regard themselves as the main sources of expertise on children with special needs, but recognise the benefits of using the parents as a resource. They consider that some of their expertise can be transplanted from them into the parents so that the parents can carry out some form of intervention with their children, e.g. paired reading (Topping 1986). The professional guides the parents by setting targets and assumes that the parent will want to act as a resource for their children.

Parents as a motivator and approver

This is a version of the resource model in which the parent is used to reward good progress at school or make sanctions at home for poor school behaviour. This assumes that the parent is seen as able to offer these rewards or carry out the sanctions. The exact nature of these may need to take into account ethical or health issues. It may not be sensible in the long term to reward behaviour with frequent trips to fast food restaurants but in the short term it could be very effective. Such home–school contracts are often linked to points systems which are recorded in the child's day book.

Subjective parent/objective professional

This is Hornby's (1995) preferred model:

> Teachers are viewed as experts on education and parents are viewed as being experts on their children. It involves the sharing of expertise and control to provide the optimum education for children with special needs. It is based upon mutual respect.
>
> The parents are viewed as being the best advocates for their child but that can lead to subjectivity which is countered by the professionals' objectivity.
>
> It does not preclude interventions based upon any of the other models.
>
> (Hornby 1995)

The problem is that professionals despite their best endeavours are not totally objective. They are subject to constraints and priorities governed by their line managers and the resources they wish to employ or avoid as value judgements based upon their past experiences and training.

Equally, while parents usually want the best appropriate provision for their children, they are not the always the best advocates for their children. We have noted that parents involved in self-help groups for parents of children with special educational needs can develop impressive skills in advocating another parent's case to a school or LEA, yet they find it very difficult to achieve the same effect when it is their child. In which case, they therefore try to get their spouse or another parent in the group to advocate for them.

It may also be arrogant to assume the professional is more of an expert on education for a child with special needs than her or his parents. The parents will have been involved in their child's special education provision since its inception over a number of years. They may have shared their experiences with parents of children with similar needs and have worried about the exact nature of their child's needs and whether or not they are being met. They might have even read books, seen videos or been on courses about their child's needs.

The SENCO, educational psychologist, case worker or advisory teacher will usually be at least as knowledgeable as the parent, but it cannot always be assumed.

These suggested models of partnership represent the variety of involvement that occurs over time between parents and different professionals. The range of involvement is dependent upon the importance and difficulty of decisions that have to be made. It is also dependent upon the parents' perception of their ability to contribute as well as their perception of the value of their contribution. If:

- things are going along swimmingly parents may just want to know that;

So which is this year's model?

35

- some important decisions are to be made about changes to provision then a parent will want to be informed and involved if they think they can have an influence;
- things are not going well and the parent thinks they do not have a voice, they will not bother.

Whole school policy on parent–teacher partnership

Parent–teacher partnership to meet special educational needs needs to be seen as an elaboration and extension of existing arrangements for partnership. However, in some schools it has been the good practice in meeting special needs that has helped to improve partnership at a whole-school level.

The key elements of a whole-school policy on parent–teacher partnership are listed in the boxed text on 'Information, partnership and access'.

> School based arrangements should ensure that assessment reflects a sound and comprehensive knowledge of a child and his or her responses to a variety of carefully planned and recorded actions *which take into account the wishes, feelings and knowledge of parents at all stages.*
>
> (DFEE 1994a, 2:28)

This stresses that the voice of parents needs to be actively sought and acted upon. 'The school based stages should therefore utilise parents' own distinctive knowledge and skills and contribute to parents' own understanding of how best to help their child' (DFEE 1994a, 1:29). Thus that the active involvement of parents is central to a child's progress.

Possibilities and pitfalls

It is important that parental involvement to meet the special needs of their child is built upon existing structures for the participation of parents in the life of the school. Some schools have adopted policies of limiting or filtering information to parents, for example providing simplified versions of IEPs or only giving positive feedback about a child's progress. Such approaches might be expedient in the short term, but may damage the long-term partnership with the parents. Parents might complain that the school has misled them or refrained from giving them the full story.

When a child's parents speak little or no English or Welsh, their involvement in process needs more active support. The school needs to investigate what information is available in the languages of the local community. The LEA and community based organisations often provide these resources including audio and video tapes which help explain what provision is available for the child and advise the parents on their role in the process.

The school might feel inclined to blame parents who are reluctant to become involved in their child's education. Nevertheless it is important not to interpret this as disinterest or apathy. Instead the

Information, partnership and access

The Code of Practice requires that the school's policy for parental involvement must outline arrangements for working with parents under three main headings:

Information

- on the school's SEN policy;
- on the support available for children with special educational needs within the school and LEA;
- on parents' involvement in assessment and decision making, emphasising the importance of their contribution:
  - on services such as those provided by the local authority for 'children in need',
  - on local and national organisations which might provide information, advice or counselling.

Partnership

- arrangements for recording and acting upon parental concerns;
- procedures for involving parents when a concern is first expressed within the school;
- arrangements for incorporating parents' views in assessment and subsequent reviews.

Access for parents

- information in a range of community languages;
- information on tape for parents who may have literacy or communication difficulties;
- a parents' room or other arrangements in the school to help parents feel confident and comfortable.

(DFEE 1994a, 2:33)

From Blamires, M., Robertson, C. and Blamires, J. (1997) *Parent–Teacher Partnership*. London: David Fulton Publishers.

school should encourage and support the parents as far as possible and advise them that their involvement can only result in the best provision for the child.

Building effective procedures for providing information

Research by Broadfoot (1989) leads to six criteria for information needed by parents. It should be:

- *objective*: comments which can be substantiated rather than based upon speculation;
- *constructive*: information which suggests strategies for improvement;
- *significant*: information which focuses on important areas of development;
- *succinct*: comments which are brief and to the point;
- *goal related*: information which can be related to parents' goals for their children;
- *broadly based*: information which gives a broad view of their children's needs.

This presupposes that the school staff know the parents' goals for their children and which areas of development are seen as being important by parents. These may be common but they might just be different.

The requirements within the Code of Practice for information to parents can be responded to as follows. Information:

- on the school's SEN policy: this needs to avoid or explain jargon and document how special needs are addressed within the school;
- on the support available for children with special educational needs within the school: this should explain how parents can register their concerns. Consider including the name of the SENCO and the name and telephone number of the special needs governor with information on their involvement in assessment and decision-making processes;
- on the support available for children with special educational needs within the LEA: most LEAs produce booklets on their support and specialist services such as speech therapy or occupational therapy and may also provide additional information for parents;
- on local and national voluntary organisations which might provide information, advice and counselling: local branches of national parents' disability groups may be able to provide support and guidance for parents. Many national organisations also provide leaflets that will be useful to parents in understanding how their children's needs may be met. LEA-instigated parent partnership projects may also be able to provide information for parents and advice on how they may be involved;
- explanation of special needs and the Code: the DFEE booklet *Special Educational Needs – A guide for parents* is freely available in a number of community languages. The Video *One in Five*

introduces the school-based stages of the Code from a parent's perspective and is available from Coventry LEA with sign language interpretation and in a number of community languages.

As stressed repeatedly in this book, schools need mechanisms for recording concerns expressed by parents and need to show that they are acting on them:

> Is there a genuine agreement with the key assumption that the school should work with parents – or are there influences (staff room chat for example) that 'put down' parents and engender a 'them and us' atmosphere?
>
> (SENJIT 1995)

Building effective procedures to register and respond to concerns

The development activities on communication blocks at the end of this book may be useful in developing active listening skills with parents. It has been suggested that teachers are good at communicating but sometimes they are not too good at listening. Active listening is:

> making a real attempt to understand what the other person is saying and the feelings behind the words, to summarise this understanding and check it out before asking further open questions that will help you arrive at a clear grasp of the problem.
>
> (Gross 1996)

There are a number of other communication skills that have been outlined in other books, e.g. Hornby (1995). Some of them are useful particularly for dealing with conflict and some may be useful for nervous parents. There might be a slight danger of becoming so adept at using communication skills that 'frank and open' discussion is lost. As Bob Monkhouse has quipped 'If you can fake sincerity, you have got it made!'

Teachers can try to persuade parents to express their views by:
- adopting a frank and open attitude to parental involvement;
- ensuring that parent concerns are heard and responded to;
- encouraging parents to bring a friend, other parent or representative from a local organisation to review meetings;
- encouraging parents to share information about their child and their concerns with the school and providing ways for the parents to find out about their child's progress;
- providing alternatives to the usual parent–teacher meeting where parents can discuss ways in which they can support their child;
- providing Curriculum Differentiation workshops for parents, which encourage parental involvement;
- building up a library of materials and games that parents can borrow to help their child (some are listed under Packages at the end of this book).

Building effective procedures for communication

Self-review: meetings

When they occur they need to be efficiently managed so that they are oriented towards solutions rather than to the attribution of blame:

- Are parents aware of the purpose of the meeting?

- If it is a formal meeting such as an annual review, are the parents provided with copies of any documents that others will have had ? (In the case of the annual review this is a requirement.)

- Are parents informed in advance about who will be attending and why?

- Are flexible times and venues arranged for meeting to take into account the parents?

- Are all the people who need to be at the meeting included?

- Are staff going to be at the meeting who do not really need to be there?

- Have you informed the parents that they may bring a friend or supporter to the meeting?

- Have you arranged for the meeting to take place in comfortable surroundings with a table so that people can place their papers?

- Are staff welcoming and approachable before and during the meeting?

- Do staff directly involved have evidence of the pupil's work?

- Are staff able to demonstrate that they understand the requirements of the special needs procedures they will be discussing with parents?

- How are parents reassured that decisions have not already been made or that the discussion started before they arrived?

- Are targets agreed upon and dates set for the next meeting?

 From Blamires, M., Robertson, C. and Blamires, J. (1997) *Parent–Teacher Partnership*. London: David Fulton Publishers.

At Stage Two and beyond of the Code of Practice an IEP is put into operation which specifies:
- the nature of the child's learning difficulties;
- action: the special education provision;
- staff involved, including frequency of support and involvement of external agencies as appropriate;
- specific programmes/activities/materials/equipment;
- what help can be given from parents at home;
- what the targets are and when they should be reached;
- how progress is monitored;
- the date of the next review meeting – usually within a term;
- who will be involved in the next meeting to discuss progress.

The IEP is more than a piece of paper. It is the forward planning needed to ensure that appropriate targets have been set and that the right help is given in order to address the child's needs.

Most SENCOs have worked with colleagues and parents to make the IEPs in their schools come alive despite resource limitations. They have trained and supported learning support assistants to understand different approaches to special educational needs and in some cases have instituted special teaching programmes for identified children.

Parents should beware of IEP's of the following kind:

INVISIBLE
Child's name appears on the register at Stage Two or Three but there are no records of any IEPs having been drawn up or used (also known as imaginary).

EXPEDIENT
Drawn up retrospectively to indicate strategies which have been used relating to either grouping or teaching arrangements. These IEPs frequently materialise immediately prior to a request for statutory assessment or a parents evening.

IMPOSSIBLE
These contain so many targets that only a superhuman (SENCO or support staff) could achieve the progress required.

USELESS
The targets on these IEPs are either so vague or so specific as to be meaningless within the stated timescale. These are often derived from equally meaningless objectives on section 7 of statements.

(Harrop 1996)

Building effective procedures for individual educational plans

41

Here are some questions that parents might want to raise about the IEP for their child which guide staff in providing information about IEPs:
- What progress has been made towards the targets?
- How are the targets monitored by staff?
- How is the child involved in monitoring her or his progress towards the targets?
- How relevant were the targets to child's needs?
- Do the targets focus upon the strengths of the child?
- To what extent does the IEP help the child to become involved with the life of the school?
- How useful was my contribution to the plan?
- How is the child feeling about school and the progress that has been made?
- Parents may want to suggest new priority targets based upon any changes, worries or developments in their child's life.

Building effective procedures for dealing with conflict

Both OFSTED and the Code of Practice require schools to have procedures in place to register and respond to parental complaints:
- if procedures for dealing with parent concerns are aimed at prevention rather than crisis management most conflicts can be avoided or limited;
- most conflict is caused by lack of information and unrealistic expectations held by either party. Clarification of roles and recognition of frustrations will help in avoiding potential conflict;
- if a school has clearly documented information on how it responds to special needs as outlined above, this can be referred to to indicate what the school has done and can do and where responsibility is then transferred to other agencies such as the LEA;
- similarly, parents can ensure that they know what the school should be doing by referring to information supplied by the school and cross checking this with information from the DFEE or national organisations. They could also contact a local support group to check their interpretation.

Building effective practice at the LEA level: the role of the Named Person

Phillipa Russell (1996) suggests that the role of Named Person as originally intended within the act was 'very unrealistic':

> We were looking for individuals with all the personal charisma of the Angel Gabriel, the patience of Solomon, the encyclopaedic knowledge of a High Court Judge and the availability of the Automobile Association.

She suggests that the role of the Named Person should depend upon the needs of the parents and that there is a need to address:
- What is the 'job description' of the Named Person?
- How are Named Persons recruited, trained and supported?
- How the Named Person relates to schools and the LEA.
- That different parents need different levels of support from the Named Person.

What do Named Persons actually do?

- they can listen to parents and encourage them to be confident and realistic in expressing their views;

- they can help parents to draw up a profile of their child;

- they can make phone calls, arrange, attend meetings with parents and draft letters;

- they can help the parents to understand the role of the different professionals and the actual assessment process;

- they can offer constructive criticism;

- they can ask the questions that parents find too difficult and accompany parents on school visits;

- they can be a befriender/enabler and offer emotional as well as practical support;

- they can help parents to access the wider voluntary sector (many children with special educational needs do not have a single identifiable disability and hence no natural link to a single voluntary organisation);

- they can provide feedback/monitoring for the LEA about relevant local issues.

(from the Parent Partnership Scheme Network)

From Blamires, M., Robertson, C. and Blamires, J. (1997) *Parent–Teacher Partnership*. London: David Fulton Publishers.

Appendix 1

Institutional Development Materials

Self-review: information

Whole-school policy on information

Does the school's special needs policy avoid unnecessary jargon and explain key terms?

Comments:

Action required:

Could the information and communication from the school convey unintended blame or criticism which might cause resentment?

Comments:

Action required:

From Blamires, M., Robertson, C. and Blamires, J. (1997) *Parent–Teacher Partnership*. London: David Fulton Publishers.

Does it outline how special needs are addressed through IEPs at Stages Two and Three of the Code?

Comments:

Action required:

Is information available to parents which enables them to register a concern?

Comments:

Action required:

Is the name and role of the SENCO in assessment and decision-making processes mapped out in relation to IEPs?

Comments:

Action required:

Is information provided on the support available for children with special educational needs within the LEA?

Comments:

Action required:

 From Blamires, M., Robertson, C. and Blamires, J. (1997) *Parent–Teacher Partnership*. London: David Fulton Publishers.

Is the information available in the language that the parents speak or are arrangements in place for the translation of this information?

Comments:

Action required:

Are booklets and leaflets produced by relevant specialist services such as speech therapy or occupational therapy made available to parents?

Comments:

Action required:

Are parents made aware of local and national branches of voluntary organisations which may be able to provide support and guidance concerning particular needs?

Comments:

Action required:

Are parents aware of LEA and parent instigated advocacy and partnership projects that exist locally?

Comments:

Action required:

From Blamires, M., Robertson, C. and Blamires, J. (1997) *Parent–Teacher Partnership*. London: David Fulton Publishers.

Self-review: whole-school policy on parental access

Are the parents aware that their child is on the SEN register and what this means?

Comments:

Action required:

Are the parents able to attend meetings about their child?

Comments:

Action required:

From Blamires, M., Robertson, C. and Blamires, J. (1997) *Parent–Teacher Partnership*. London: David Fulton Publishers.

Does the school provide transport or crèche facilities for parents who have these difficulties which prevent them from attending meetings in school?

Comments:

Action required:

Do the parents inform the school of their concerns and aspirations for their child?

Comments:

Action required:

From Blamires, M., Robertson, C. and Blamires, J. (1997) *Parent–Teacher Partnership*. London: David Fulton Publishers.

Do the parents contribute to the setting of priorities for meeting their child's needs?

Comments:

Action required:

Do parents acknowledge the information given about their child's special needs?

Comments:

Action required:

From Blamires, M., Robertson, C. and Blamires, J. (1997) *Parent–Teacher Partnership*. London: David Fulton Publishers.

Can the parents support their child in meeting his/her special educational needs?

Comments:

Action required:

Do they encourage and reward their child's progress towards targets?

Comments:

Action required:

From Blamires, M., Robertson, C. and Blamires, J. (1997) *Parent–Teacher Partnership*. London: David Fulton Publishers.

Are they able to work on particular targets at home?

Comments:

Action required:

Self-review: communicating with parents

Do teachers adopt a frank and open attitude in their involvement with parents?

Comments:

Action required:

Do staff listen to parent concerns expressed and respond to them?

Comments:

Action required:

 From Blamires, M., Robertson, C. and Blamires, J. (1997) *Parent–Teacher Partnership*. London: David Fulton Publishers.

Does the school encourage nervous or unsure parents to bring a friend, other parent, parent governor or representative from a local organisation along to meetings to ensure that the parent remembers to ask all the questions they want to and register all their concerns in meetings?

Comments:

Action required:

Does the school provide alternatives to the usual parent–teacher meeting to discuss ways in which the child can be supported?

Comments:

Action required:

Have staff reviewed the communication skills they use with parents so that they are not perceived as attributing blame?

Comments:

Action required:

Has the school reviewed the format of the information that it gives to parents so that it is understandable and efficient?

Comments:

Action required:

From Blamires, M., Robertson, C. and Blamires, J. (1997) *Parent–Teacher Partnership*. London: David Fulton Publishers.

Does the school have a parent support group or actively link in with local parents support networks?

Comments:

Action required:

An example questionnaire sent to parents by an OFSTED inspection team

I feel the school encourages parents to play an active part in the life of the school

Strongly agree   Agree   Neither   Disagree   Strongly disagree

I would find it easy to approach the school with questions or problems to do with my child(ren)

Strongly agree   Agree   Neither   Disagree   Strongly disagree

The school handles complaints from parents well

Strongly agree   Agree   Neither   Disagree   Strongly disagree

The school gives me a clear understanding of what is taught

Strongly agree   Agree   Neither   Disagree   Strongly disagree

The school keeps me well informed about my child(ren)'s progress

Strongly agree   Agree   Neither   Disagree   Strongly disagree

The school enables my child(ren) to achieve a good standard of work

Strongly agree   Agree   Neither   Disagree   Strongly disagree

The school encourages children to get involved in more than just their daily lessons

Strongly agree   Agree   Neither   Disagree   Strongly disagree

I am satisfied with the work that my child(ren) is/are expected to do at home

Strongly agree   Agree   Neither   Disagree   Strongly disagree

The school's values and attitudes have a positive effect on my child(ren)

Strongly agree   Agree   Neither   Disagree   Strongly disagree

The school achieves high standards of good behaviour

Strongly agree   Agree   Neither   Disagree   Strongly disagree

My child(ren) like(s) school

Strongly agree   Agree   Neither   Disagree   Strongly disagree

60   From Blamires, M., Robertson, C. and Blamires, J. (1997) *Parent–Teacher Partnership*. London: David Fulton Publishers.

Different schools' responses to their identified development needs:

- *School One*
  A small primary school set up a library of games and other materials that parents could borrow to help their children;

- *School Two*
  A secondary school provided a number of curriculum workshops for parents to learn how to support their children's homework in different lessons;

- *School Three*
  Provided the DFEE (1994b) booklet *Special Educational Needs: a guide to parents*, which is freely available in a number of community languages to parents who had been informed that their children were on the special needs register. They followed this up with an invitation to come into school to watch with other parents the Coventry LEA video *One in Five,* which is also available in a number of community languages as well as having signed interpretation;

- *School Four*
  A large urban secondary school encouraged parents of children with special needs to drop in for coffee before school on their way to work or when they dropped their children off;

- *School Five*
  Encouraged parents to share strategies that they found useful in addressing pupils' needs at the IEP meeting which they then suggested to other parents as appropriate;

- *School Six*
  Set up a self-help group for parents of children with special needs on the register of the school which shared concerns but also had input from local voluntary groups and advisory teachers and specialists to discuss concerns, strategies and interventions.

From Blamires, M., Robertson, C. and Blamires, J. (1997) *Parent–Teacher Partnership.* London: David Fulton Publishers.

Appendix 2

Development Activities

Case studies

These case studies are intended to help teachers and parents understand the different viewpoints and priorities that each might have to arrive at some common course of action. Try to identify:

What hopes and ambitions might the parents have for their child?	
The parental concerns:	The school's concerns:
Common ground:	Differences:
Any further information that may be needed:	
The next steps for the parents:	The next steps for the school:

From Blamires, M., Robertson, C. and Blamires, J. (1997) *Parent–Teacher Partnership*. London: David Fulton Publishers.

Reception: Rachel

Rachel is four years old. She has Down's syndrome. Rachel has attended a local playgroup with a one- to-one helper for the past year. She has some language (about twenty words) and is beginning to learn to dress herself. In the playgroup setting Rachel enjoys playing with the other children and listening to stories. Although not completely toilet trained Rachel has made good progress. The playgroup supervisor reports that Rachel sometimes argues with the other children over toys and that she spits when she talks. Rachel's parents are keen for her to attend a mainstream school and the local mainstream school has been suggested, although the statement of special educational needs has not been finalised. Rachel's mother feels that the local school is not prepared to welcome Rachel and has a negative view of her. She is afraid that, 'Rachel has failed before she has even started, they seem scared to death of the idea of a child like her in their school.' Rachel's parents have requested a meeting with the headteacher who has asked the SENCO to attend.

Primary: Dean

Dean is nine. Until he was seven he loved school but since then he has been more and more reluctant to get ready in the morning. He often has tantrums after school and finds it hard to get to sleep at night. Dean tells his mother that the work at school is too hard but his teachers have always been pleased with his work and say he is near the top of the class in most areas. His mother suspects that Dean has dyslexia as his father who is dyslexic describes having similar problems at school. Because of his mother's concern Dean has been put at level one on the audit but his teacher maintains that there is no indication of a learning problem. He does well in his spelling tests and behaves well at school although he is a bit of a 'perfectionist'.

Secondary: Thomas

Thomas is eleven. He has a statement of special educational needs because he is dyspraxic. The statement, which was completed just before the end of his last term at primary school, says he should have a lap-top computer and ten hours per week one-to-one classroom support. He is finding the amount of homework he is given very difficult to complete and is generally unwilling to go to school each morning. Thomas's mother has spoken to the SENCO who told her that the provision in the statement is only a *recommendation*. There is no lap-top for Thomas to use and as far as his mother can discover he is not getting any one- to-one help.

From Blamires, M., Robertson, C. and Blamires, J. (1997) *Parent–Teacher Partnership*. London: David Fulton Publishers.

Example parent–staff development session

Teacher–parent partnership

Description and aims of the session	An outline of the Code's requirements for partnership with parents with an opportunity to consider the parents' views and review the response of the school
Speakers and tutors	SENCO, headteacher, LEA representative (parent partnership scheme), local support group
Introduction: **What are special needs?** **Outline of stages of the Code** **How parents can be involved** **The school's response** **How help is given** **What information is available** **How parents can access the school** **How parents help their child** **How the school can help parents**	It may be useful to use the Coventry Video funded by the DFEE and then follow up with summary OHP's within this document and produced by the LEA or school Your notes:

Ideas for action and follow up as a result of this meeting:

Access: **Communication:**   **Partnership:**

From Blamires, M., Robertson, C. and Blamires, J. (1997) *Parent–Teacher Partnership*. London: David Fulton Publishers.

Avoiding blockages to communication

Comment

Certain phrases can hinder conversation between professionals and teachers or may develop a confrontation. While we advocate a 'frank and open' exchange of views between both parties, tact and diplomacy do have a role to play. If the partnership is robust then it may well be appropriate to use one or two of these phrases. However, we leave it to you to decide which phrases are best never uttered.

The following activity should be helpful for staff discussing their experiences of talking with parents. This activity has been developed from ideas suggested in an article by Jean Gross (1996).

Talking with parents

Say	Instead of saying...	Why
	'I don't know why you are worried. He is doing as well as expected.'	
	'She'll grow out of it!'	
	'She tends to be lazy.'	
	'He can be quite disruptive.'	
	'There's lot worse than him – so we can't give him extra help.'	
	'She is not dyspraxic/dyslexic/ADD etc.'	
	'We do not accept the private assessment of your daughter's needs.'	
	'He is just not motivated.'	
	'What do you expect from a child with her background?'	
	'Your child's difficulties are more to do with his attitude than his learning difficulty.'	
	'Your child has made little progress so it would be pointless to invest in any more provision.'	
	An example from your own experience.	

From Blamires, M., Robertson, C. and Blamires, J. (1997) *Parent–Teacher Partnership*. London: David Fulton Publishers.

Talking with parents: possible answers

Say	Instead of saying ...	Why
Can you tell me why you are worried?	'I don't know why you are worried. He is doing as well as expected.'	This avoids invalidating their views.
Let's see what we can do about it.	'She'll grow out of it!'	This recognises that the parent has a concern.
She takes quite a bit of motivating. What is she interested in at home?	'She tends to be lazy.'	This avoids the negative label a bit and seeks to explore what can be done.
He can be quite disruptive when he settles down to work if he is unsure of what to do.	'He can be quite disruptive.'	You may well feel you can say this but then you need to explore possible solutions.
We need to be clear about what targets will be most helpful and what we can do together to help.	'There's lot worse than him – so we can't give him extra help.'	This again is dismissive of the parents' view.
Let's take a close look at her difficulties and strengths. What have you noticed?	'She is not dyspraxic/ dyslexic/ADD etc.'	The label battle is best avoided by refering to exact needs and strengths.
The LEA has the responsibility for statutory assessment but you are able to request that a statement is considered and your report could be included as evidence but in the meantime ...	'We do not accept the private assessment of your daughter's needs.'	The parents may need more information about the Code of Practice as well as reassurance that the school is responding to their obvious concern in an appropriate way.
I'd really like to know what can spark his interest.	'He is just not motivated.'	This is another version of 'He is a lazy kid'.

From Blamires, M., Robertson, C. and Blamires, J. (1997) *Parent–Teacher Partnership*. London: David Fulton Publishers.

We need to look closely at what she likes doing as well as the difficulties she has at school.	'What do you expect from a child with her background?'	Practically, anything could be said instead of this witting or unwitting slur.
He doesn't appear to be happy at school. How is he at home? What does he want to do after school?	'Your child's difficulties are more to do with his attitude than his learning difficulty.'	You are avoiding saying that he is a sulky kid and seeking ways to get him interested.
We need to look again at the support we are providing so that it can be made more effective.	'Your child has made little progress so it would be pointless to invest in any more provision.'	Admit when something is not working and try to change it rather than give up.
	An example from your own experience	

From Blamires, M., Robertson, C. and Blamires, J. (1997) *Parent–Teacher Partnership*. London: David Fulton Publishers.

Initial perceptions of parents

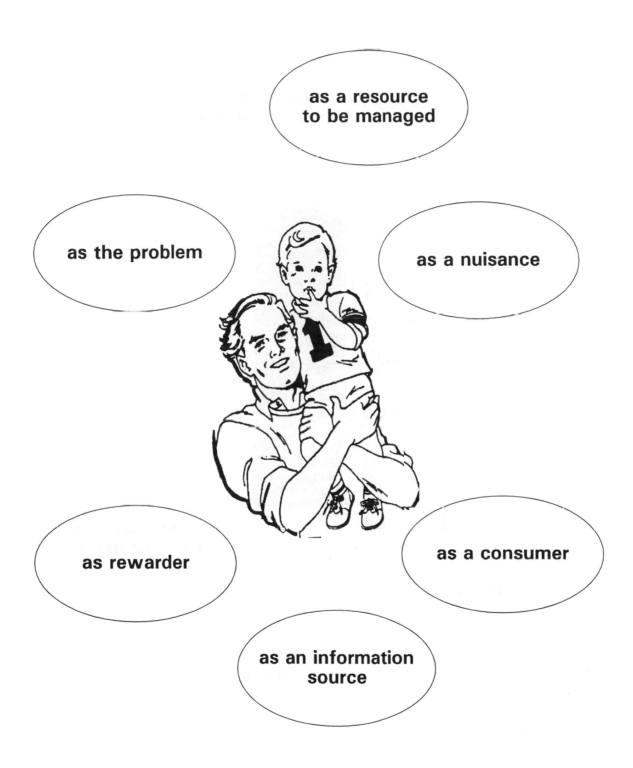

as a resource to be managed

as the problem

as a nuisance

as rewarder

as a consumer

as an information source

From Blamires, M., Robertson, C. and Blamires, J. (1997) *Parent–Teacher Partnership*. London: David Fulton Publishers.

Initial perceptions of teachers

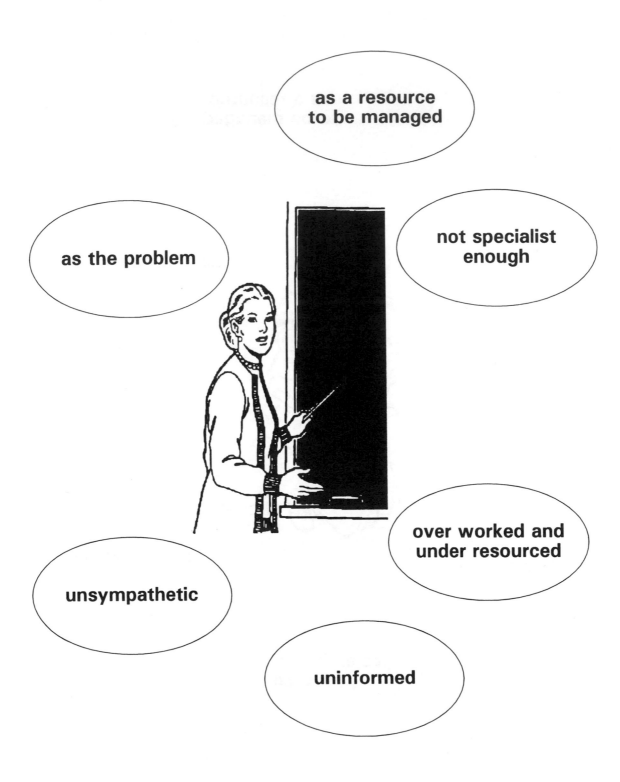

as a resource to be managed

as the problem

not specialist enough

over worked and under resourced

unsympathetic

uninformed

From Blamires, M., Robertson, C. and Blamires, J. (1997) *Parent–Teacher Partnership*. London: David Fulton Publishers.

Challenges for parents of children with special educational needs

Parents of children with special needs are seen as needing to address a series of tasks, each of which must be mastered at least partially if they are to come to terms with the situation.

(Hornby 1995)

1) Parents must accept the reality of their child's special needs and come to terms with their own reactions to the situation and to the reactions of family, friends and the wider community.

2) Parents must gain an understanding of the nature of their child's special needs and learn skills for facilitating the child's development.

3) Parents need to learn how to access relevant health, education and welfare services and establish working relationships with the professionals involved with their child.

4) Parents need to learn how to participate appropriately in decision-making regarding their child's educational placement, medical treatment, future training and work placement.

5) Parents need to identify individuals and groups who can provide them with support and to build up a support network.

6) Parents must establish a positive parenting relationship and learn to cope with the day-to-day tasks of caring for their child with special needs.

7) Parents must be able to maintain their self-esteem despite the difficulties they encounter, and maintain a positive relationship with their partner in order to establish a balanced family and personal life.

8) Parents must be able to accept their children's right to independence, such as the expression of their sexuality and their need to live outside the family home.

9) Parents must organise provision for their children with special needs for the future when they may become ill or die.

10) Parents must be able to help the child understand his or her disability and adapt to living in the community.

(Hornby 1995)

From Blamires, M., Robertson, C. and Blamires, J. (1997) *Parent–Teacher Partnership*. London: David Fulton Publishers.

73

How parents can help their child and their school

This list is not intended to make parents feel guilty about the amount of help they give their children. Parents will be doing most of these things without realising it anyway. The list just gives suggestions to help parents think about how they help their children to learn.

	Quite a lot	Sometimes	Not much	What can be done
Making decisions Keep children's work and information from school in a folder				
In touch with the school/ teacher				
Fill in and return forms sent home by the school				
Read the home-school diary or reading record				
Contact the teacher if children cannot do homework or if you are worried about progress or provision				
Talk with other parents about the school				
Attend meetings for parents				
Tell the school staff about parents' needs, ideas and concerns				
Go to school events such as sports days, plays and ceremonies				
Offer to help in the school or on school trips when you have the time				
Supporting children Make sure children get a good night's sleep				
Make sure children have breakfast				
Make sure they attend school unless they are ill				
Talk and listen to them every day about what is happening at school				

From Blamires, M., Robertson, C. and Blamires, J. (1997) *Parent–Teacher Partnership*. London: David Fulton Publishers.

	Quite a lot	Sometimes	Not much	What can be done
Encourage them when they are finding something difficult at school				
Praise them when they have been successful at school				
Learning Read and tell stories with younger children				
Provide a time and quiet place for homework				
Let children help you with chores in the home so that they can gain new skills				
Talk about anything and everything with your children				
Watch television together and talk about the programmes				
Read newspapers, magazines and books and talk about them to show that reading is important				
Ask the school how you can help your child's learning				
Play games together especially those that require thinking				
Other ideas				

From Blamires, M., Robertson, C. and Blamires, J. (1997) *Parent–Teacher Partnership*. London: David Fulton Publishers.

Helping parents prepare for an IEP meeting

Below are some questions for you to think about in preparation for the IEP meeting. However, your choice of questions will obviously be informed by your knowledge of the child:

- What do you feel are the strengths of your child?

- What do you feel are your child's weaknesses (e.g. areas that may be frustrating or that you feel your child has a particular need to improve in)?

- How do you think your child learns best? (What kind of situation makes learning easiest?)

- Please describe educational skills that your child practises at home regularly (e.g. reading, making crafts, using the computer).

- Does your child have any learning or behavioural difficulties that are of concern to you or other family members? If so, please describe them.

- What are your child's favourite activities?

- What are your child's special talents, hobbies and interests?

- Does your child have any particular fears? If so, please describe.

- How does your child usually react when upset and how do you deal with the behaviour?

- Do you have any particular concerns about your child's progress at school? If so, please describe.

- What are your main hopes for your child this year?

- Is there other information that would help us gain a better understanding of your child?

- Are there any concerns that you would like to discuss at the next IEP meeting?

Thank you for contributing valuable parental insights.

Sincerely

_____

(Special Educational Needs Co-ordinator)

 From Blamires, M., Robertson, C. and Blamires, J. (1997) *Parent–Teacher Partnership*. London: David Fulton Publishers.

Glossary

Code of Practice   a guide to schools, parents and LEAs about the help they can give children with special educational needs.

Educational psychologist   a psychologist usually employed by an LEA who is an expert on learning and emotional difficulties.

GEST (Grant for Educational Support and Training)   a grant made by the DFEE to LEAs to pay for identified priorities in training teachers.

Parent   any person who has care of the child or who is not the natural parent of the child but has responsibility for him or her.

Mainstream school   an ordinary school.

Note in lieu of a statement   a note by which an LEA will give its reasons not to make a statement after statutory assessment.

Special educational needs (SEN)   a child has special educational needs if he or she has a learning difficulty that needs special educational provision.

Special educational needs coordinator (SENCO)   the teacher who is responsible for coordinating special educational needs provision within the school.

Special educational provision   the special help that is given to a learner with special educational needs.

Special school   a school which is specially organised to make special educational provision for pupils with special educational needs and is approved by the Secretary of State.

Statement of special educational needs a document that sets out a child's needs and the frequency, location and provider of the help that he or she should get.

Statutory assessment a detailed examination of a child's special educational needs which may lead to a statement.

Organisations

ACE Centre
Ormerod School
Wayneflete Rd
Headington
Oxford OX3 8DD

Tel: 01865 63508

Provides expertise in the use of microelectronics as aids to communication. Staff are involved in the assessment of individual children in collaboration with schools and parents.

Action for Sick Children
Argyle House
29–31 Euston Rd
London NW1 2SD

Tel: 0171 833 2041

Concerned with the support of parents and children with severe medical conditions.

ADD Information Services
Argyle House
PO Box 340
Edgware HA8 9HL

Tel: 0181 958 6727

Sells books and videos and provides advice on Attention Deficit Disorder.

Advisory Centre For Education
18 Aberdeen Studios
22 Highbury Grove
London N5 2EA

Tel: 0171 354 8318

Produces a wide range of publications and guides many relating to the legal aspects of special education.

AFASIC (Overcoming Speech Impairments)
347 Central Market
Smithfield
London EC1A 9NH

Tel: 0171 236 3632/6487

Advice and support through regional groups for parents and teachers of children with language disorders including semantic and pragmatic language problems.

Association for Brain Damaged Children
47 Northumberland Rd
Coventry CV1 3AP

Tel: 01203 25617

Association for Spina Bifida and Hydrocephalus
Ashbah House
42 Park Road
Peterborough PE1 2UQ
Tel: 01733 555988

Basic Skills Agency
1–19 New Oxford Street
London
WC1A ANU

Tel: 0171 405 4017

Formerly ALBSU, the Adult
Literacy and Basic Skills Unit now
works with schools to develop basic
skills.

British Diabetic Association
10 Queen Anne Street
London W1M OBD

Tel: 0171 323 1531

British Dyslexia Association
98 London Road
Reading RG1 5AU

Tel: 01734 66271

British Epilepsy Association
Anstey House
40 Hanover Square
Leeds LS3 1BE

Tel: 01532 439393

**British Sports Association
for the Disabled**
Hayward House
Barnard Crescent
Aylesbury
Bucks HP21 OPG

Tel: 01296 27889

Brittle Bone Society
Ward 8
Strathmarine Hospital
Strathmarine
Dundee DD3 OPG

Tel: 01382 817771

CENMAC
Eltham Green Complex
Middle Park Avenue
London SE9 5HL

Tel: 0181 850 9229 Fax: 0181 850 9220

email: cs33@cityscape.co.uk

Provides expertise and advice in the
use of IT as a resource for access and
communication.

**Centre for Studies on Inclusive
Education**
1 Redlands Close
Elm Lane
Redland
Bristol BS6 6UE

Tel: 0117 923 8450

**Centre for Studies on Integration
in Education**
4th Floor
415 Edgeware Rd
London NW2 6NB

Tel: 0181 452 8642

Publishes a number of free and
inexpensive leaflets and reports on a
range of disabilities and learning
difficulties to help parents and
professionals.

Children's Legal Centre
20 Compton Terrace
London N1 2UN

Tel: 0171 395 6251

Runs free advice service 2–5 pm on
all aspects of law and policy
affecting children and young
people. Publishes a range of
guides including a monthly
Childright magazine.

The Children's Society
Edward Rudolph House
Margery Street
London WC1X OJL

Tel: 0171 837 4299

Part of the British Computer Society
Disability Interest Group. Provides
advice on special needs devices and
software for children and adults.

Computability Centre
PO Box 94
Warwick
CV34 5WS

Tel: 01926 312847

Free phone for private individual
enquiries: 0800 269545

Contact a Family,
170 Tottenham Court Road,
London W1P OHA

Tel: 0171 383 3555

Very useful resources for parent
partnership plus information about
rare conditions.

Council For Disabled Children
c/o National Children's Bureau
8 Wakely Street
London EC1V 7QE

Tel: 0171 278 9441

Cystic Fibrosis Research Trust
Alexandra House
5 Blyth Road
Bromley
Kent BR1 3RS

Tel: 0181 464 7211

DFEE
Department For Education and
Employment
Sanctuary Buildings
Great Smith Street
London SW1P 3BT

Tel: 0171 925 5000

Publishes the following free guides.
*Code Of Practice on the Identification
and Assessment of Special Educational
Needs: Special Educational Needs: a
guide for parents* and *Special
Educational Needs Tribunal: how to
appeal*, available by phone: 01787
880946.

**(Nationwide Telephone
Information and Advice Services)
DIAL UK**
117 High Street
Clay Cross
Derbyshire

Tel: 01246 250055

**Disability Alliance
ERA**
1st Floor East
Universal House
88–94 Wentworth Street
London E1 7SA

Tel: 0171 247 8763

Disabled Living Foundation
380–4 Harroe Road
London W9 2HU

Tel: 0171 289 6111

Down's Syndrome Association
155 Mitcham Road
London SW17 9PG

Tel: 0181 682 4001

**Dyslexia Computer Resource
Centre**
Department of Psychology
University of Hull
Hull HU6 7RX

Tel: 01482 465599

Family Fund
Joseph Rowntree Memorial Trust
PO Box 50
York YO1 1UY

Tel: 01904 621115

Friedreich's Ataxia Group
The Common
Cranleigh
Surrey GU8 8SB

Tel: 01483 27274

**Further Education Funding
Council**
Cheylesmore House
Quinton Road
Coventry CV1 2WT

Tel: 01203 863000

Concerned with the work of FE
colleges in the UK.

**GLAD (Greater London
Association for Disabled People)**
336 Brixton Road
London SW9 7AA

Tel: 0171 274 0107

Haemophilia Society
123 Westminster Bridge Road
London SE1 7HR

Tel: 0171 928 2020

Handicapped Adventure Playground Association
Fulham Palace
Bishops Avenue
London SW6 6EA

Tel: 0171 736 4443

Huntington's Disease Association
108 Battersea High Street
London SW11 3HP

Tel: 0171 223 7000

Hyperactive Children's Support Group
71 Whyke Lane
Chichester
Sussex PO19 2LD

Tel: 01903 725182

I CAN
Barbican City Gate
1–3 Dufferin Street
London EC1Y 8NA

Tel: 0171 374 4422

Provides courses and information on children with speech and language difficulties.

In Touch
10 Norman Road
Sale
Cheshire M33 3DF

Tel: 0161 962 4441

Information about rare handicapping conditions

IPSEA (Independent Panel for Special Education Advice)
22 Warren Hill Road
Woodbridge
Suffolk IP12 4DU

Tel: 01394 382814

Provides advice and support for parents going to tribunals.

Kids
80 Wayneflete Square
London W10 6UD

Tel: 0181 969 2817

Leukaemia Care Society
PO Box 82
Exeter
Devon EX2 5DP

Tel: 01392 218514

MENCAP
117–123 Golden Lane
London EC1Y ORT

Tel: 0171 454 0454

Support for parents of children and adults with learning difficulties.

MIND
22 Harley Street
London W1N 2ED

Tel: 0171 637 0741

Motability
Gate House
West Gate
The High
Harlow
Essex CM10 1HR

Tel: 01279 63566

Muscular Dystrophy Group of Great Britain
7–11 Prescott Place
London SW4 6BS

Tel: 0171 720 8055

NAGM (National Association of Governors and Managers)
Suite 36/38
21 Bennetts Hill
Birmingham B2 5QP

Tel: 0121 643 5787

NASEN (National Association of Special Educational Needs)
NASEN House
4 and 5 Amber
Business Village
Amington
Tamworth
Staffordshire B77 4RP

Tel: 01827 311500

National Association for the
Education of Sick Children
Open School
18 Victoria Park Square
London E2 9PF

Tel: 0181 980 6263

National Autistic Society
276 Willesden Lane
London NW2 5RB

Tel: 0181 451 1114

A source of advice on the education
and needs of children and adults
with autism and Asperger
Syndrome

National Deaf Children's Society
45 Hereford Road
London W2 5AH

Tel: 0171 229 9272

National Eczema Society
4 Tavistock Place
London WC1H 9RA

Tel: 0171 388 4097

**National Federation for the Blind
of the United Kingdom**
Unity House
Smyth Street
Westgate
Wakefield
West Yorkshire WF1 1ER

Tel: 01924 291313

**National Federation of Access
Centres**
Hereward College of FE
Bramstom Crescent
Tile Hill Lane
Coventry

Tel: 01203 461231

Provides services aimed at increasing access in further education for
students with disabilties through
the appropriate use of microelec-
tronic devices. Includes research
and training as well as assessment.

**National Library for the
Handicapped Child**
Ash Court
Rose Street
Wokingham
Berks RG11 1XS

Tel: 01734 89110

National Portage Association
4 Clifton Road
Winchester
Hants

Tel: 01962 60148

Portage is an intervention programe
for young children with disabilities
which places a high emphasis on the
parents' involvement.

National Rathbone Society
1st Floor
Princess House
105–7 Princess Street
Manchester M1 6DD

Tel: 0161 236 5358

Support, advice and provision for
young adults with learning difficulties.

National Toy Libraries Association
68 Churchway
London NW1 1LT

Tel: 0171 387 9592

**NCET (National Council for
Educational Technology)**
Milburn Hill Road
Science Park
Coventry CV4 7JJ

Tel: 01203 416994

Provides a range of publications
and courses on the use of IT across
all phases of education.

Network
16 Princeton Street
London WC1R 4BB

Tel: 0171 831 8031/7740 (advice
service)

Network 81
1–7 Woodfield Terrace
Chapel Hill
Stansted
Essex CM24 8AJ

Tel: 01279 647415

Supporting parents wanting integrated education for their children.

Neuro-Fibromatosis Association
120 London Road
Kingston upon Thames
KT2 6QJ

PHAB (National Physically Handicapped and Able Bodied)
Padholme Road East
Peterborough
Cambridgeshire PE1 5UL

Tel: 01733 54 117

Parents in Partnership
Unit 2
Ground Floor
70 South Lambert Road
London SW8 1RL

Tel: 0171 735 7733

A parental support group for parents of children with special educational needs.

RADAR (Royal Association for Disability and Rehabilitation)
12 City Forum
250 City Road
London EC1V 8AF

Tel: 0171 250 3222

Royal National Institute for the Blind
224 Great Portland Street
London W1N 6AA

Tel : 0171 388 1266

Royal National Institute for the Deaf
105 Gower Street
London WX1E 6AH

Tel: 0171 387 8033

SCOPE
12 Park Crescent
London W1N 4EQ

Tel: 0171 636 5020/0800 626216

(Helpline 1–10pm)

Formerly the Spastics Society serving children with Cerebral Palsy and their parents.

SENSE
11–13 Clifton Terrace
Finsbury Park
London N4 3SR

Tel: 0171 272 7774

Dealing with needs of people who are blind or partially sighted and deaf.

Sickle Cell Society
54 Station Road
London N4 3SR

Tel: 0171 272 7774

SNUG (Special Needs User Group)
39 Eccleston Gardens
St Helens WA10 3BJ

Tel: 01744 24608

A regional support group for teachers and parents using IT to meet special educational needs. They have a lot of inexpensive software for the BBC/PC for SEN.

Special Education Consortium
c/o Council for Disabled Children
8 Wakely Street
London EC1V 7QE

Tel: 0171 278 9441

Spinal Injuries Association
Newpoint House
76 St James Lane
London N10 3DF

Tel: 0181 444 2121

Stroke Association
CHSA House
Whitecross Street
London EC1Y 8JJ

Tel: 0171 490 7999

Tuberous Sclerosis Association of Great Britain

Little Barnsley Farm
Milton Road
Catshill
Bromsgrove
Worcs. B61 0NQ

Tel: 01527 871898

Young Minds
22a Boston Place
London NW1 6ER

Tel: 0171 7262

Packages

Parenting skills

Wilmslow
Markets a range of videos on parenting skills. A number are focused on early years.

Wilmslow
Telford Rd
Bicester
Oxon OX6 OTS
Tel: 01869 244733

Teaching

These packages can make limited resources go further. They can be used by parents or learning support assistants to provide a framework for meeting identified targets:

Toe by Toe
A highly stuctured multi-sensory reading method within a workbook of exercises lasting twenty minutes per day which is widely regarded to overcome reading difficulties and dyslexic-type problems.

8 Green Road
Baildon
Shipley
West Yorks. BD17 5HL
Tel: 01274 598807

THRASS (Teaching Handwriting and Spelling Skills)
A structured intervention method for children with difficulties in this area uses audio cassettes, workbooks and progress charts.
Collins Educational
HarperCollins Publishers
FREEPOST GW5078 Bishopbriggs
Glasgow G64 1BR

Information

One in Five: a parents guide to special educational needs
A useful video narrated by a somewhat gushing Toyah Wilcox available in most community languages and British Sign Language.

Public Relations Unit
Coventry City Council

Tel: 01203 833333

The Basic Skills Agency
Produces a range of resources to support the development of numeracy and literacy (address in the organisations section).

Software

NCET produces guidance on the use of computers to support learners with special educational needs (address in the organisations section).

SNUG has a range of inexpensive software for special educational needs for PCs and BBC (address in the organisations section).

REM (Tel. 01458 253636) produces a catalogue of special needs software.

References

Armstrong, D. (1995) *Power and Partnership: parents, children and special educational needs*. London: Routledge.

Broadfoot, P. (1989) 'Reporting to Parents on Student Achievement: the UK experience', Working Paper No. 2/89 (October), Bristol University.

CACE (1967) *Children and their Primary Schools*. Plowden Report. London: HMSO.

Carpenter, B., Ashdown, R. and Bovair, K. (Eds) (1996) *Enabling Access: effective teaching and learning for pupils with learning difficulties*. London: David Fulton.

Dale, N. (1995) *Working with Families of Children with Special Needs*. London: Routledge.

DES (1978) *Special Educational Needs*. Warnock Report. London: HMSO.

DFEE (1994a) *The Code of Practice for SEN*. London: HMSO.

DFEE (1994b) *Special Education Needs: a guide for parents*. London: HMSO.

DFEE (1994c) *Special Educational Needs Tribunal: how to appeal*. London: DFE Publications.

DFEE (1994d) *Our Children's Education: the updated Parents' Charter*. London: HMSO.

Dyer, C. (1995) 'The Code of Practice Through LEA Eyes', *British Journal of Special Education*, **22**(2).

Gascoigne, E. (1995) *Working with Parents as Partners in SEN*. London: David Fulton.

GRIDS (1988) *Guidelines for Review and Internal Development in Schools: primary school handbook*. Second edition. London: Longman for the School Curriculum Development Committee. (Note, a secondary school version is available.)

GRIDS (1989) *External Perspectives in School-based Review*. London: Longman for the School Curriculum Development Committee.

Gross, J. (1996) 'Working with Parents', *Special Children*, May.

Harrop, J. (1996) Communications to the NCET SENCO email forum archives held at mailbase.ac.uk.

Hornby, G. (1995) *Working with Parents of Children with Special Needs*. London: Cassell.

Moses, D. and Croll, P. (1985) 'Parents as Partners or as Problems', *Disability, Handicap and Society*, **2**, 75–84.

Norwich, B. (1996) 'Special Needs Education or Education for All: connective specialisation and ideological impurity', *British Journal of Special Education*, **23**(3).

OFSTED (1995a) *Guidance on the Inspection of Nursery and Primary Schools.* London: HMSO.

OFSTED (1995b) *Guidance on the Inspection of Secondary Schools.* London: HMSO.

OFSTED (1995c) *Guidance on the Inspection of Special Schools.* London: HMSO.

Russell, P. (1996) Paper presented at the DFE/National Children's Bureau Day Conference, marking two years of the Code of Practice.

SENJIT (1995) Discussion Papers, Special Education Needs Joint Initiative in Training, London Institute of Education.

Stobbs, P., Mackey, T., Norwich, B., Pearcey, N. and Stephenson, P. (1995) *Schools' Special Educational Needs Policy Pack.* National Children's Bureau Enterprises Ltd.

Topping, K. (1986) *Parents as Educators: training parents to teach their children.* London: Croom Helm.

Wolfendale, S. (1992) *Parental Partnership.* London: Cassell.

Wragg, T. and Brighouse, T. (1995) 'A New Model of School Inspection'. School of Education occasional paper, Exeter University.